THE SELLER
OF SECRETS

THE SELLER OF SECRETS

A MEMOIR

KATHLEEN ROSE MORGAN

SHE WRITES PRESS

Published 2024
Printed in the United States of America

Print ISBN: 978-1-64742-678-1
E-ISBN: 978-1-64742-679-8
Library of Congress Control Number: [LOCCN]

For information, address:
She Writes Press
1569 Solano Ave #546
Berkeley, CA 94707

Interior design and typeset by Katherine Lloyd, The DESK

She Writes Press is a division of SparkPoint Studio, LLC.

Names and identifying characteristics have been changed to protect the privacy of certain individuals.

CONTENTS

For those who remain lost
in the darkness of shame
and the bitterness of somber secrets

"A book must be the axe for the frozen sea within us."
—Kafka

PROLOGUE

It was difficult to imagine how my journey to learn the truth about what happened to me could lead to the discovery of secrets more appalling than the enduring and insidious memories that rarely left my thoughts. These memories kept me from complete amnesia, and although I disregarded them with great effort, they will undoubtedly remain forever etched into my bones. For me, survival was a creative act of ignorance until I ran out of ingenuity and was pulled from its dark and lonely recesses. Unable to hold back my secrets any longer, I came face-to-face with my unspoken trauma when truth burst from my lips at the end of a routine day. With a hefty dose of courage, I untangled the woven layers of shadow that kept the details of my memories hidden. I became determined to make sense of my wounds and uncover the truth of what lurked in the foggy haze of my repressed memories. I made progress in stages, taking my efforts to heal in a deliberate and gentle manner until I received shocking information that led me to scrutinize my ongoing research amid the debris of the past. After four years of healing work and a fresh start in a new state, I was shattered by an end-of-life confession from Mother as she faced the fear of uncertainty only death can bring.

As the end of life nears, a transformative process often begins and prompts one to review the events that occurred during one's lifetime by reflecting on the good times, the bad times, and the roles played within both. For those who have committed cruelties or crimes and who have held secrets and misdeeds, it becomes clear that the end of life may be a final chance to lift the silence and alleviate burdens of guilt and regret—one's last chance to clear the conscience before moving on to the great unknown.

The deathbed confession may be seen as an opportunity to absolve sins or as a last-ditch effort to save one's soul. It teeters between courageous and cowardly. For those of the Catholic faith, like Mother, it is believed that confessing your sins to a priest will allow God to forgive them and permit your soul to enter heaven. As Mother's health was deteriorating, in the absence of a priest, she chose Roseanne, the director of the care home where she resided.

Are we all worthy of the opportunity for redemption at the end of our lives? For people who have led immoral and destructive ones, will resistance to redemption remain, or will the fear of death soften even the hardest of hearts and make one beg for mercy?

Although Mother held many secrets during her life, in the end, she would not forego the final opportunity to seek forgiveness and relieve herself of undoubtedly her most vicious one. At the time of Mother's confession, the effects of dementia were causing her to believe the past was the present.

Memory is not one process of the brain but a complex set of various structures. In dementia patients, the perception of time and the function of memory are disorganized. Short-term memory can be impaired while long-term memories remain intact. Many can remember events that took place decades ago, while unable to recall what happened earlier the same day, and some live fully in the past. Childhood events are well encoded in the brain, and the effects of post-traumatic stress disorder (PTSD) can appear in those who have repressed painful memories. Traumatic memories can emerge to be relived over and over, and it is possible to become, to some extent, trapped in those memories.

This often results in an added diagnosis of depression and is treated as a form of psychosis.

During the year between Mother's confession and her death, her dementia increased in intensity to the point where she did not remember the past or the present. It was her greatest gift. Despite our lifelong disconnected and difficult relationship, I remained her caretaker not only toward the end when she resided at the care home but throughout her life since my childhood. During a routine monthly check-in, Roseanne and I planned to discuss Mother's upcoming move to a facility capable of providing the advanced medical care she needed as her health deteriorated. After our usual friendly exchange via text message, Roseanne began a conversation that would change my life forever:

> She has been having a tough time. The dementia is progressing, but she is still aware of me, the girls, and the other residents; she still knows the basics but seems to be living in the past. I am guessing there may have been some bad times in her life, and she has some regrets. She is often depressed and cries.

This statement did not surprise me, and I sadly felt a sense of satisfaction. I had never been able to shake off the past, but I thought Mother would never crack. She was the rubber, and I was the glue. Things were different now, though, and my intense demand for the truth led me to wonder if this might be an opportunity to get answers. I had a clear understanding Mother revealed something to Roseanne. I trusted her and tried to lead the conversation toward finding out what she knew.

I took a deep breath and typed:

> A long time ago, something bad did happen, and I was trying to find forgiveness when I picked her up and brought her to Vermont. Dementia brought her back to how she treated me as a child. She

was mean. Her behavior was extreme and erratic. It was my reason for finding a residence for her immediately. She needed more help than I could give. I must ask you, Roseanne, did she mention anything during her time with you about what happened in the past? I have been waiting for her to tell me the truth my whole life. I am afraid it may be too late now.

As I paced back and forth in my backyard, the crisp early spring chill was not just from the still-cool weather. As I stared into the forest bordering the property, an uneasy feeling stirred within me as I watched the ellipsis blink and waited for the words to appear on the screen. After several minutes they emerged:

I hate to say this, but it has been a difficult week. Yesterday was a bad day. She was crying and carrying on all about you. She said she did something bad and you would never forgive her. She said they made her do it. She said she loved you and she was sorry. She kept repeating how she didn't do anything to stop them from hurting you. She said she knew this was why you did not want to see her. The girls told her you loved her and that, whatever happened, you forgave her a long time ago. I had to take her to her room because she was so upset and upsetting everyone else. She couldn't stop crying. She was hysterical. I asked everyone to leave so I could get her calmed down. She did say something to me, but I don't know if you want to hear it, Kathleen.

I was ready. I wanted the truth. Finally, her admission of guilt for helping to cover up what happened to me in the rectory. I had recently been fighting a repulsive feeling she may have dropped me off that day knowing what was going to happen. She told Roseanne "they" made her do it. She did not stop "them" from hurting me. I read those words again. They sent a shudder down my spine. I braced myself and typed:

I do, Roseanne.

I took deep breaths again and prepared to hear the truth about what happened that day, thirty-six years ago, which had altered the trajectory of my already-fragile young life and permanently marked my subsequent days with its dire consequences. The ellipsis appeared, and I watched as it faded in and out. My mind raced in wonder until the words appeared:

> She said to me that she took you to bed with her and did things to you. Things you will never forgive her for. She told me that she was abused too. It started when she was a young girl. Her life was ruined and instead of protecting you, she let it happen to you too, and worse, she helped them. I am so sorry to say this to you, Kathleen. I am heartsick for you, honey.

I read the text repeatedly. I could not direct my brain to make sense of those shocking words. My breathing became shallow. Nauseous and dizzy, I entered the forest and leaned against a tree. I sank to the ground on weak legs and closed my eyes. I knew the feeling of being in shock and this was surely it. I took deep breaths. What words could convey the feeling I was left with from this grotesque statement? I responded:

> Thank you for having the courage to tell me. I assume the "them" are the pedophile priests she hand-delivered me to when I was around eleven or twelve years old. Well, this explains a lot. Did she say anything else?

I used every tool I had learned about healing over the last four years within those few minutes to gain control of my emotions. I could not lose this chance to know more. I needed to know the whole truth. I had hoped Mother had taken this opportunity to get everything out in the open, but Roseanne's response ended the possibility.

No, that was all she said, Kathleen. She just kept repeating she was a horrible person. You would not believe what I did. I did horrible things for them. I am so sorry, honey.

The shock of her confession churned into a pure and vibrant rage in the pit of my stomach. I had no tears, only grave and solemn anger, which I allowed to take over my entire being. My body was tense and wedged against the sturdy tree. I stared into the forest. It was awakening from a long winter's sleep, with the first hint of warmth transforming the landscape with foliage and budding wildflowers. Yet there I sat, frozen in disbelief and anger.

I reviewed the text messages from the beginning again, thinking I might have misinterpreted the words. I went back to read a third time when Roseanne's final message appeared:

I will pray for you to find peace in your heart, Kathleen. I am sure her actions changed the person you are or could have been. She knows what she did. I am sure she has paid the price for it in many ways. You have a beautiful family. Be as happy as you can be every day. Life is fleeting. You wake up one day older than you want to be and wasted days when you could have been happy. I know this from my own experience, honey. Sending you big hugs.

I had briefly considered that learning whatever information Roseanne had to share would be the end of my inquiry into what had happened to me, but it was just the beginning. I knew this confession was merely a small piece of a larger story. It would also prompt a gradual release of my blocked recollections and an intense demand in my heart for accountability.

Just months before Mother's confession, I had been gifted

with the ability to seek justice by filing a civil lawsuit against the Archdiocese of New York and related defendants through the newly passed Child Victims Act. After learning of her hideous actions, I inquired as to whether Mother could be added to the list of defendants. Due to her dementia diagnosis, she could not. Still, she had provided important clues about the dysfunction I was born into. These clues became the catalyst for the path I set out on to uncover what happened. I was determined to know the whole truth. And in the end, what I learned was even darker and more heartbreaking than I ever could have imagined.

Chapter One

IT'S A GREAT LIFE
IF YOU DON'T WEAKEN

Stories are powerful. They play a vital role in our collective and personal development. Entire cultures have passed on traditions and folklore through storytelling. Stories have the power to evoke empathy and compassion, allowing the reader to see the world through another's eyes. Stories can be healing. Every story we learn makes emotional connections in our hearts and minds, giving us opportunities to develop understanding and appreciation for others. Stories educate us on topics we may not otherwise be familiar with. We can find meaning in stories, especially those told by others with shared experiences. Our personal story shapes our identity and is referenced throughout life. It affects our physical and mental health. Our story determines our self-worth, level of risk-taking, confidence, shame, or guilt. Our stories are encoded in our genes and passed down through generations. Healing the story of a traumatic past can reconcile history and rewrite stories to a more just ending. Sharing stories of truth with love and understanding effectively supports personal power, healthy relationships, and community healing for the greater good of the human spirit.

This is my story. It is the story of my heroine's journey. A journey of reclaiming the parts of myself lost through adversity, embracing a new way of life to make peace with the past, and finding the wisdom in my wounds. I began writing it down as a form of therapy. At first, I could just write a sentence or two. Writing the words was as hard as saying them aloud.

"Writing is cathartic," said Jennie, my expressive-arts counselor, who suggested I use writing to give voice to unspeakable words.

"Cathartic" means "providing psychological relief through the open expression of strong emotions; causing catharsis; having to do with purging the body." It is true. Writing is cathartic, and once I realized its positive impact, I wrote every day. The words that formed the descriptions of what had happened to me shaped my scattered glimpses of memory. Each sentence flushed the toxic effects of trauma and secrets out of my body and onto the page. My secrets had been stored away in an abstract space I formed in my childhood psyche for so long that acknowledging them was like opening a time capsule of nightmares. I had to pretend the nightmares were not real. Years later, repressed memories would be explained to me as "emotional grenades." It was only a matter of time before something snagged a pin and one of them detonated, blowing me to smithereens.

Once my pin got snagged, the ensuing explosion caused a violent blast and a declaration of truth shot out of my mouth. Just one, at first. After the initial rupture, I released the rest of the truth over time. In a slow drip, I shared my true story with the person closest to me. I shed the lies I wrapped around myself like a protective shield. My true story was rooted in the muteness of shame and dissociation. But now the truth was released, and I was cloaked in its salacious narrative.

Writing transformed from catharsis into an intense pursuit of truth and healing. In researching my history and the serendipitous path I traveled as I grew, where I found deep resilience through mentors and creative pursuits after the worst of it was over, I became cognizant of how I am so much more than what happened to me. Writing allowed me to reshape my story into a more authentic one.

Intuitively, I always knew I would tell this story. Still, I anxiously wrestled with every facet and every outcome until it became clear that I had to just tell the truth, even when all others had abandoned it. I realized that if I did not tell this story, it would be my deathbed confession.

Standing within the heaviness of my unearthed wounds, I stepped further into my journey and into an investigation of my past with a focus on identifying the root cause of the dysfunction that marked my life. To fully shed the dense weight of trauma, I needed to know why such misery flourished and how it choked the lives of those around me. I knew there was much more I needed to learn to free myself from years of silence and the collective unexpressed grief and fear I still carried. The deep-rooted, unresponsive old systems of indifference had to be explored, healed, and restored. To do this, I had to start at the beginning.

Staten Island, one of the five boroughs of New York City, is geographically connected to New Jersey at its west; it's bordered by the tip of lower Manhattan and Brooklyn at its north and, at its east, by the great expanse of the Atlantic Ocean, the path my ancestors traveled to the United States as Italian immigrants in the late nineteenth century. Rather than the teeming and overcrowded tenements in Manhattan or the Bronx, they settled in an area of the North Shore of the Borough of Richmond called New Brighton, named in honor of the resort town of Brighton, England. There was a rich history here.

By the time my ancestors arrived, the land, farms, and surrounding forests and vegetation once tended by the original inhabitants, the Lenape, were buried by concrete and development. Beginning in 1834 and conceived by wealthy real estate developers and other entrepreneurs, the land was set up to further develop and promote the area as a summer retreat to lure wealthy Manhattanite high society. They built an elegant summer getaway with quaint cottages and stately Victorian mansions, many of which are landmarked for preservation today. The fashionable summered here and enjoyed swimming, boating, glamourous balls, and fresh air outside of the city. Lawn tennis was introduced in America at newly built athletic clubs on the waterfront during this period.

Although just 5.2 miles from Manhattan by ferryboat, the Borough of Richmond was a world away from the crowded city. New Brighton was incorporated in 1866 as one of six wards in the town of Castleton. In 1861, the onset of the Civil War resulted in large changes to the neighborhood's land use, and residential real estate became in high demand. Water and sewage systems were developed in the late 1800s, followed by the settlement of several immigrant groups, which quickly urbanized the village. In 1898, the Borough of Richmond was consolidated with New York City. The area thrived due to its fast-growing economy thanks to the large manufacturing plants built on the waterfront, which employed many residents. By the end of the 1920s, some of the borough's first large apartment buildings and three- and four-family dwellings were erected to house the increasing population. It was not until 1975 that the Borough of Richmond's name was changed to the Borough of Staten Island.

On the waterfront, the Kill (the Dutch word for "stream") Van Kull met the Hudson River, and this well-situated location transformed into a bustling area for manufacturing and trade use as the Industrial Revolution took hold. Over time, the quaint summer retreat of the wealthy became a toxic area beset by poor air quality from pollution, illegal dumping, and contamination from the many cargo ships and tankers delivering goods to New

York City and New Jersey for distribution throughout the country. Manufacturers of plaster and Sheetrock and chemical plants filled the area and leaked toxic substances into the air, land, and water. The emergence of production and commerce brought with it the destruction of the environment and adversely affected the health of the area's inhabitants and workers. New Brighton became a concrete landscape mixed with industry, taverns, and residential housing.

Toxicity has a way of spreading through air, water, soil, food, and even DNA transmission, generation to generation.

Beginning in the mid-1970s, the closing of factories brought job loss but also ceased the further spread of toxins. The construction of housing projects developed affordable but segregated housing, and the area saw an increase in poverty and today would be known as an economically challenged food desert.

The most egregious toxification of the area came from the role Staten Island played in the Manhattan Project, the 1939 research and development of nuclear weapons during World War II led by the United States with support from Canada and the United Kingdom, in response to the fear of Hitler's Germany using nuclear technology to develop weapons. Scientists were examining uranium and plutonium in facilities set up in several locations around the United States and Canada, with most of the work and testing performed in a Los Alamos laboratory in northern New Mexico. The Atomic Age was ushered in on July 16, 1945, when the first atomic bomb was detonated, creating a forty thousand–foot mushroom cloud in the desert 210 miles south of Los Alamos, causing considerable damage to nature and human health.

The high-grade uranium ore needed for the project was mined in the Belgian Congo and purchased by the United States. In 1938, twelve hundred tons of uranium stored in 2,007 steel drums were delivered by tanker through New York Harbor, along the Kill Van Kull, and stored in a linseed oil manufacturing plant just over two miles from New Brighton. Although it was called the Manhattan Project, Staten Island was tasked with storing the radioactive materials. The Archer Daniels Midland building, located adjacent to the Bayonne Bridge connecting Staten Island to Bayonne, New Jersey, would store the uranium for three years until it was loaded onto railcars and transported to Los Alamos. It is still not known whether the drums leaked upon arrival or departure. The secrecy behind the country's effort to produce the world's first atomic bomb kept the possibility of a radiation leak hidden for over fifty years until a local community leader investigated after hearing a rumor about radioactive contamination, which, by the 1990s, was no more than an urban legend.

On a Saturday in May 1971, I was born in this place, joining a family who masqueraded as ordinary (a skill I also grew to acquire and master the art of) but who were truly nothing short of remarkable failures. Mother was an emotionally damaged woman shrouded in depression and dark secrets. Father was a man plagued by alcoholism, and by noble yet failed attempts at impeding further harm to his family from said secrets, who lived in a state of drunken evasion for many years before jumping ship. I merged with an extended bloodline and community plagued by toxic male aggression, submissive women, wannabe Mafia brutes, charlatan holy men and women, and lurid and criminal goings-on, which were all made possible by cheek-turners, complicit and fearful enablers, and an ever-present, overarching code of silence.

Ten months after my birth, stricken with severe pneumonia, I almost died in the same hospital where I was born. I spent several weeks there, and at one point during my stay, the doctors told my family to say their goodbyes, as it seemed I would not survive. Of all the stories I have heard of my early years, this might be the only true one. It was the only story whose details did not change over time when it was told. Further validation came much later in life when I found the hospital bill from March 1972, addressed to Father for $1,372.91, a fortune in those days for our modest family.

Today, I wonder if I had changed my mind about what I signed up for in this human existence and attempted to make a dash for it.

Mother was born in 1931 amid the Great Depression, the fifth of ten children born to my grandparents. A clear and stark disconnection existed between us of which I was always acutely aware. Her lack of tenderness was upsetting and puzzling until I became mature enough to comprehend how the circumstances of Father leaving may have led to her disposition. Still, the only views my young mind could connect to her strange demeanor were distressing ones, like how she never offered the standard motherly love, which seemed to come naturally to other mothers whom I witnessed or saw on television. She was not a hugger or a particularly warm person. She was different, often angry, and often sad. She talked to herself all the time, smoked cigarettes, and read bad romance novels, the kind with a shirtless man riding a horse on a beach with a woman in a willowy dress nearly collapsing over his manly greatness on the cover. She occasionally attended Thursday-night bingo games at my school but otherwise did not socialize much.

From an early age, I was her only confidante, her sounding board, and the main recipient of her petulant complaining and deep want for pity related to the circumstances she found herself in after Father left when I was a toddler. In response, I tried to avoid her, learning to withdraw into an alternate place where I was alone and where I developed a deep yearning for attention, affection, and love. Her confusing rhetoric grew stranger as I matured, and through her ramblings, she taught me to not trust anyone and to never expect that I deserved the feeling of security and other prerequisites to a peaceful life. She taught me to understand how men were superior to women and that I should be in their service. She taught me to be quiet and small. She trained me in the art of closed-minded, jealousy-driven commentary and taught me never to be curious about learning any lesson other than that life is hard and disappointing.

As I matured, I wondered if she had an undiagnosed mental illness, but as a child, I feared her and feared for her. My greatest hope was that I might one day wake up to a normal, caring mother. Instead, tasked with being her caretaker and sympathizer, she brainwashed me directly and indirectly to serve her through psychological abuse and manipulation.

Many mornings, I would awaken from the sound of whispered talking coming from the kitchen. As a small child, I would lay in bed and listen, making out a few words: "He said he would. . . . She is something else. . . . If I had the money to . . . Oh well, you get kicked in the ass again, Mother. . . . It's a great life if you don't weaken."

I wondered who came to visit so early in the morning. With the anticipation of seeing whoever it was she was talking to, I jumped up and walked into the kitchen only to find no one there. Mother sat at the kitchen table alone. I asked who she was talking to, and she denied she was talking at all and said I must have been hearing things.

Each time, it seemed like I heard a conversation with all the ingredients of a back-and-forth exchange between two people. At times, she stopped talking if she heard my footsteps approaching. Often, she did not hear me approaching, and as I grew and listened from behind the wall, I learned small pieces of details, which began to shape the million-piece puzzle I have been constructing ever since. It was a recurring situation and became so common I learned to ignore it, put on the television to cover her whispers, or put my fingers in my ears to muffle them. Mother was undeniably alien to me, and I became convinced that something had gone wrong with my arrival on earth and I'd ended up in the wrong family.

Memories of my childhood were held in fractured glimpses until I emerged from my forgetting and inspected them thoughtfully and with purpose. Looking through old family photographs over the years, I have yet to find one of Mother holding me as a baby or throughout childhood. Not one. No holiday or school events. No random family photos. None. This detail served to validate my sense of being unwanted by her.

During times with extended family, when stories were being shared around the dinner table at a wedding or other gathering, there were always stories told of how my grandparents would take me upstairs to their apartment often. They would take me out of my crib without a word. Now, I understand how they offered me an otherwise-absent connection to love, safety, and relationship. Gifting me these important early bonds created space for crucial resiliency.

Mother never had any interest in or passion for anything, just the simple drudgery of day-to-day happenings . . . no want for knowledge or conversation beyond the weather and what she was scraping together for dinner. She gave up on life long before I was born and lived in a stark and sad world. The visceral disconnection between us left me without a clear identity and sense of self.

Father was born in 1933. I did not know much about him other than the terrible words Mother spewed into my ears and the few little-remembered interactions of my own. I was the only one of his children with the same hazel-colored eyes he had. This made me feel out of place in my family. I was a blonde-haired, hazel-eyed girl in a family of brown-haired, brown-eyed people. No one looked like me because I looked like him.

What I did know about Father I learned in passing from others over time and from my own research. I knew he worked for several years at a Sheetrock factory and later became a bus driver for the City of New York with a route through our neighborhood. I had been told when I was born that he stopped the bus in front of our apartment building and kept the passengers waiting, so he could hold me for a minute or two. I had been told he was handsome and kind, one who would "give you the shirt off his back." I had been told he was an artist and skilled at sketching portraits and landscapes.

In researching my past and the father I never knew, I requested information from the National Personnel Records Center to learn more about his military service. The letter I received in return explained a fire in 1973, which destroyed a major portion of the records of US Air Force personnel with surnames beginning with letters from *H* to *Z* for the period 1947 through 1963. I was provided with basic information through alternate record sources, but a complete copy could not be reconstructed. I learned he joined the air force when he was seventeen years old and served as an Airman Third Class during the Korean War. He enlisted in June 1951 and trained for ten weeks at F. E. Warren Air Force Base outside of Cheyenne, Wyoming. He was assigned to the 812th SUPRON Strategic Air Command (SAC) bomber unit. SAC B-29s had flown over 21,000 raids and dropped 167,000 tons of bombs during the war. Thirty-four B-29s were lost in combat and forty-eight B-29s were lost to damage or crashes, taking many young lives with them.

After the cease-fire on July 27, 1953, he returned to Walker Air Force Base in Roswell, New Mexico, which had been acquired by the US Air Force for flight testing and aircraft and weapons testing. He was discharged in June 1955 and returned to Staten Island. He later received the Korean Service Medal, the UN Service Medal, and the National Defense Service Medal.

He married Mother just a few months after his return in October 1955. As an adult, I learned she was three months pregnant at the time. They had two children one year apart. I arrived fourteen years later, and soon after, it all collapsed. From a tender age, Mother programmed and brainwashed me into believing Father was a terrible person who did not care about me at all. As a child, all I understood about the situation was how Father stuck around until my siblings were older, but soon after I arrived, he left.

Throughout my childhood, I had hoped Father may reconsider and take me to live with him. On occasion, I was told I would be seeing him and waited at the window for him to come and pick me up, dreaming he kept me and never returned me to Mother. He showed up a few times, but most of the time he did not, and I was left to stare out the window. Mother did not ever alleviate or lessen my sorrow. According to her, he was a drunk and did not care about me at all. He only cared about his new wife and her daughter. Mother groomed me for many things; one was to hate Father, who left me just like he left her.

She did not work throughout their eighteen-year marriage but was forced to once he left. He never sent any money. She was hired as a nurse's assistant at a local nursing home. She complained so much about having to wipe the shit off old people's asses, I believed it was specifically her job. She was a shit wiper. She wore a white medical uniform, which made it easy to tell my friends she was a nurse and helped people when they were sick.

"It's a great life if you don't weaken" was a phrase I would hear frequently from Mother, directly or indirectly, through her unrelenting self-chatter. It was her standard response to any unjust moment, her disappointment at having to be a shit wiper or any general sadness. "Do not be weak and it will not be so bad." It comes from a cartoon by Gene Byrnes with the same title, published from 1915 to 1919 in the *New York Evening Telegram*. The phrase was a rallying cry for American soldiers during the First World War. I wondered who passed the phrase to her.

My family lived in a three-story apartment building bordered by a tavern on each corner and two blocks away from the

Catholic church and school everyone attended. During my early years, my grandparents lived on the third floor and other family members on the second floor, with Mother, my two siblings, and me on the first floor. Because my siblings were teenagers when I was born, I had the sense of being an only child, even though I was not.

Each floor of the building had a clothesline hanging from the window, which stretched across the backyard to a pole where the kitchen-sink-washed clothing was hung to dry. As I grew taller, I was able to walk through the first-floor line and let the sun-dried clothes wash over me, gently caressing my head and flattening the top of my hair. It was a three-story-high ceremonial display of garments of all colors, shapes, and sizes, swaying back and forth in the breeze.

A small round pool was tucked in the corner close to the house. A swing hung from the top of the opened garage door, where I swayed back and forth listening to everyone talk. The adults smoked cigarettes, one after the other, stamping them out in huge ashtrays the size of a dinner plate. It was an artful mix of the women's red- and pink-lipstick-edged butts and the men's plain ones. I gathered leaves from the one tall tree standing on the small strip of dirt and grass, which bordered our neighbor's backyard and ours, lighting them in the open garage with matches from beside the giant ashtray. One at a time, I lit the tip and watched the leaf burn until it was just ashes. I swept the ashes with the edge of the matchbook cover into little piles, creating a pattern to walk through.

I spent most of my time in my grandparents' apartment stretched out on the black-and-white linoleum kitchen floor in front of the stove watching my grandma make gravy. "Gravy," the New York City Italian American word for tomato sauce.

One of the great linguistic debates, the gravy-sauce dispute is a matter of semantics akin to belonging. The English word "sauce" sounds like the Italian word *salsa*. Italian immigrants wanted to fit in and be American so using the word "gravy" was an attempt at using a more American word. Also, the gravy goes on top of macaroni, not pasta. Another debate for another time.

I loved listening to the sound of my grandma chopping cloves of garlic and onions on a thick cutting board. I counted each time the knife hit the hard wood and waited with anticipation for the loud sizzle of the pieces as they were dropped into the heated olive oil in a pot so big, I could curl myself up and fit my whole body in it. The aroma quickly filled the apartment. She opened several giant cans of crushed tomatoes and poured them into the pot. As it cooked for what seemed like all day, we played games and watched *Mister Rogers' Neighborhood* together, my favorite television show. My grandparents were the helpers Mister Rogers told me to look for.

I have strong remembrances of sitting on my grandpa's lap and coloring at the table.

The care and love they provided to me when it was in short supply in my own home were significant. One day, my grandfather was not feeling well and asked me to sit on the chair while he went to rest. I never saw him again. I was told he went to heaven. It was winter, and I remember hoping he was not cold on the way.

My grandfather was born in 1893 and emigrated to the United States from the Campobasso region of Italy by way of Naples with his parents when he was a toddler. They settled in Staten Island. Italian immigration was flourishing during this time, with masses fleeing desperate poverty and arriving in the United States through Ellis Island. Scores of Italians settled in New York City, living in tenements in neighborhoods with other Italian immigrants. Anti-Italian sentiment was heavy because of their darker skin complexion and the assumption they engaged in misconduct or held a tendency for criminal behavior, which resulted in less protection from police patrols. This helped the Mafia, also known as the Black Hand, hold sway over the community by embezzling money from small business owners through death threats and violence.

In a twist of fate, as my grandfather returned to Italy in 1915 to visit family, his trip coincided with Italy's declaration of war on Austria-Hungary. Because he was still an Italian citizen not yet naturalized in the United States, he was immediately drafted into fighting in the First World War (1914–1918) as a soldier in the Italian army. Overall, the Italian public was not enthusiastic about the war, and the army was not ready to undertake a prolonged conflict. They hoped for a speedy conclusion and victory. He became part of a special-forces unit known as the Bersaglieri, an elite troop that sported unique uniforms, with each member wearing four hundred black feathers of a particular wood grouse known as a capercaillie fastened to his hat or helmet. This unit was an aggressive military fighting force known for their fierceness on the battlefield as well as their dramatic, high-stepping marches on parade grounds. They were noted for their sharpshooting skills and agility. The plumes on the hats provided shade for shooting and served as a form of camouflage. This tradition gave birth to the phrase "a feather in your cap," an accomplishment one should be proud of.

He fought as a soldier in the Fourteenth Regiment, Sixty-Fourth Battalion, in a series of battles. He was captured in October 1917, twelve miles north of Udine, and spent fourteen months as a prisoner of war in Austria-Hungary. Approximately six hundred thousand Italian soldiers were imprisoned in POW camps in the aftermath of the Battle of Caporetto. Poor treatment, heavy laborious work, and malnutrition prompted escape attempts in droves. Countless POWs died from pure exhaustion and disease from grim living conditions, poor sanitation, and food shortages. The war raged on, and the captured Italian soldiers were ostracized in Italy with little official relief offered to them in Austria. Soldiers who were taken prisoner by the enemy were regarded as cowards and traitors. Upon their release and return to Italy, they were held in quarantine and subjected to interrogation. Italy held no welcoming celebrations for their returning prisoners of war, not even for those who wore the elite feathers in their caps. The Italian political and military authorities' handling of its soldiers was called scandalous and shameful. A prime example of their ineptitude was the wagonload of crackers they sent to starving prisoners, which arrived after the war ended. The government worked to ensure their clumsy initiatives and responsibility for the great suffering their troops endured would be quickly forgotten.

Upon my grandfather's official discharge from the Italian army, he returned to the United States and settled back into life on Staten Island. After meeting and marrying my grandmother and starting a family, he applied for a job with the Department of Docks as a deckhand for the Staten Island Ferry, but he was turned away because he was Italian. The boat workers were mostly Irish, the other once-marginalized immigrant group who were the target of the long-forgotten "No Irish Need Apply" business ads in the newspapers of the 1850s. My grandfather did not accept their rejections and kept showing up until they eventually hired him. He worked on the ferryboat until his retirement.

A decade later, he was contacted by the Italian consulate in New York and notified he was being awarded the Silver Medal Cross and the Gold Medal of Victory, officially receiving the designation of *cavaliere*, the Italian version of knighthood given to citizens who have served their country valiantly. The *Ordine di Vittorio Veneto* was instituted with a single rank of knight "to express the gratitude of the nation" to those decorated with the Cross of War who had fought for at least six months in World War I and earlier conflicts. He spent part of the late winter and early spring in Florida attending the Yankees' spring training games and had to be convinced to cut his trip short to come back to New York to receive the medals.

The effects of battle on the mental health of soldiers, known at the time as shell shock, was attributed to exposure to artillery attacks and bombings. Popular opinion was the exhibited symptoms were the result of a concussion to the nervous system, but it did not explain the same symptoms in soldiers who had not been exposed to bombings. Instead, their exposure to the effects of war gave a diagnosis of neurasthenia or nervous breakdown. Despite the pervasiveness of soldiers experiencing shell shock, it was often attributed to weakness and cowardice, which caused many to hide their symptoms and suffer in silence, not getting the help they needed. Formal treatment for shell-shocked soldiers was primitive at best and ranged from electroshock therapy to rest. PTSD was not a diagnosis, and no standard treatment existed for it until the 1980s. The now-understood symptoms stemmed from the release of stress hormones, which provided a surge of energy in the brain.

Over time, PTSD changes the brain by causing the area that handles memory, the hippocampus, to shrink. Trauma victims are significantly more likely to experience problems controlling anger, feeling anxious, and feeling constantly on edge.

My grandfather was drafted into fighting brutal battles on the front lines of combat for a country he left when he was a baby. War and related suffering from the effects of being a POW in the mountains of Austria-Hungary left its mark. He was organized for wartime long after the war ended. He suffered with anger issues but also had a stout heart, loved animals, and loved his family. During his time in Florida, he called to talk to the dog.

The story I was told about my grandmother was how after completing elementary school, she went to work at a garment factory to help support her family. She met my grandfather, and once she turned eighteen, they married and had eleven children, one of whom did not survive. Today's availability of census data and other public records revealed the truth. My grandmother was pregnant and seventeen years old when she married. Thirty days later, she gave birth to her first child. She spent her entire life in service to my grandfather, fourteen years her senior, and to a cycle of pregnancies, births, and rearing children one after another, starting when she was a child herself. She passed away when I was ten years old. My remembrances of her evoke warm and loving feelings. She provided my sole source of resilience in my early life.

Mother dutifully followed the belief instilled in her, and many women of her day, that she would be safer, provided for, and happier if she stayed quiet and relinquished control to men. She was staunchly conditioned to see the women fighting for women's rights as adversaries who disrupted the system of conformity to the male expectations she prescribed. She remained unwaveringly cloaked in and complicit to male control throughout her life and tried to pass on adherence to this plan to me.

In our history and lineage, like many others, the women were the keepers of the land. They were the practitioners of folk medicine who made significant contributions to health and medical care in Renaissance Italy. The women were the healers and the keepers of knowledge and tradition for hundreds of years until their work became undervalued through the Catholic demotion of the feminine and their hijacking of pagan practices.

Here is where the balance shifted. It is our collective indifference that keeps it unbalanced.

Although the women in my family did not outwardly acknowledge or ever seem aware of their connection to this past, some rituals were carried on. I recall watching my grandmother reverently set a bowl of water on the table. She recited whispered prayers while adding drops of olive oil to the water. If the drops of oil formed into the shape of an eye, the *malocchio* was confirmed.

The *malocchio*, or evil eye, was brought upon a person by the envious glare of another. If one suddenly fell into misfortune or a string of bad luck, it was likely this envious glare had found you. There were ways to protect oneself from this misfortune, such as pinning a red ribbon to the lapel of a jacket or the strap of a purse. Wearing a bullhorn pendant on a necklace or using the bullhorn hand position, which to my amusement was the heavy-metal hand gesture brought to legions of fans by Ronnie James Dio's Italian grandmother, in a downward motion would serve to block the malevolent gaze of the *malocchio*. In those moments of ritual, I saw my grandmother as the woman she truly was—the defender, the healer, the wise woman, and my very own guardian angel.

In researching and trying to make sense of my own trauma, I recognized the importance of understanding how intergenerational trauma can negatively affect a family lineage. Consequences of trauma, especially in earlier generations, were rarely discussed openly but instead blocked or minimized. The only option was silence.

Through this inherited muteness, the passing down of the impact of negative emotions, damaging coping skills, and ignorance of the root cause of the trauma is circulated through the family line. Unspoken trauma is like a parasite that slowly kills its host, severs relationship cords, leaves an impression of isolation, and slips the parties into a chasm of silent grief that deepens with each passing year. It takes just one person to stop the ineffective cycles of denial and silence. The consequences of this result in passing along healthy coping skills to the next generation.

In the fogginess of my early childhood memory lives a man called The Captain. I do not remember him fully but have had glimpses of memories of him from time to time throughout my entire life. For a long while, the only recollection I had was that he lived three blocks away up the hill on the corner by the public pool.

I did not know his real name, but I knew he was important to Mother. I can recall the large garden behind his house. I would stand in a patch of tomatoes, lettuce, cucumbers, and other fruits and vegetables I did not recognize while Mother was inside. I did not know people could grow their own food; most of the food in our home came from cans or boxes. The plants grew high and over one another and were held up by tall poles, which towered over me. A concrete slab was positioned in front of the garden and raised above the soil. I stood on it so I could reach up and rub each plant's leaves between my fingers. Some were scratchy and rough; some were smooth and silky. For a time, I wondered if he would be my new dad. He was nice to Mother, and we went to the house with the garden several times. Sometimes there were other kids there with their parents and we played and hid in the garden. I was so small, it seemed I could hide behind a tomato.

During the summer of 1976, shortly before I was going to start kindergarten, the Son of Sam emerged and terrorized the city for over a year, committing eight separate shootings in different boroughs. He wrote letters to the police department, taunting them, and appeared on the front of local newspapers and on the television news. Everyone was talking about it, everyone was scared, and no one knew where he could strike next. It went on for a long time and besides the overall sense of fear, I remember my older siblings and cousins were told to not be outside at night. I was already primed for fear and the shaky uncertainty that came along with dysfunction and understood how, if I did not go outside when it was dark, the Son of Sam would not get me.

Mother's job was across the street from the school where I attended kindergarten. She walked me there in the morning. Our neighbor, the lunch lady, slipped me small containers of chocolate milk when everyone else had been given plain milk. I still drank the plain milk and hid the chocolate milk in the waistband of my pants, to hide it from the other kids. After school, Mother took me to her job, where I sat in a room and drank my prized warm chocolate milk. We walked home past the schoolyard and watched the older kids play stickball as we passed.

After the year ended, I would be going to first grade at St. Paul's. Everyone in my family and in the entire neighborhood went there, including my older siblings and cousins, and before them Mother and her siblings. I had to wear a uniform, which relieved me from having to wear my hand-me-down clothes, but I was still disappointed when I found out it was a dress, not pants. We had to take the bus to the uniform store in Port Richmond to buy shirts, dresses, and special shoes.

A powerful thunderstorm came through after we arrived home and the lights went off. Once it became dark, I thought the Son of Sam was going to show up. Everyone gathered in the backyard. I stayed inside. I sat by the window with my forehead pressed on the screen and watched as they listened to a radio broadcast explaining how the entire city was in a blackout. The lights stayed off for a long time. After they came back on, life continued as usual and the next time the electricity went out, it was not due to a blackout. It was because the bill was not paid, and I learned to understand the meaning of not enough.

Not long after my grandfather passed, everything changed. My grandmother left to live with other relatives. Soon, the last remaining family left, the apartment building was sold, and strangers moved into the top two floors. I would only see my grandmother on Sundays, when we gathered at her new house. I would sit next to her on the couch where, in warmer months, when I wore shorts, my bare legs would stick to the thick plastic covering the cushions.

I waited all week for Sunday to arrive, when I could spend time with family. I especially loved to sit in the back seat of the car of another aunt and uncle, who usually gave Mother and me a ride there and back. It was a big car with soft velvety seats I would sink right into. It was a smooth ride. I thought the car wheels must have been hovering just above the ground because it was so different from the noisy bus or bumpy taxicabs, which seemed to shed parts as they moved. The radio station always played classical music. I usually felt unsafe in cars, but not theirs.

Sometimes we had to take the bus, which I did not mind. I was used to taking it everywhere else. Mother did not drive. To get to my aunt's house, we had to take two buses and walk a long way. Sometimes we had to wait up to an hour for each one to show up. Mother would grumble the whole time about having to take the bus on a Sunday, when the schedule was different, but the prize of absorbing her grumpy complaining was to spend time with family and eat delicious food and desserts.

Outside of school, I spent most of my time alone in our apartment watching television or outside in the neighborhood with friends while Mother worked at the nursing home. In all sorts of weather, other neighborhood kids and I were outside from early morning until the streetlights came on at dusk. One favorite activity was making crayon-wax bottles. We collected matches, candles, crayons, and empty bottles. We sat in a tight circle, using our shared supplies to light the candles and steadily burn the tips of the crayons over the sides of the bottles, allowing the melted wax to drip down the sides, creating beautiful rainbows of color around the glass.

Across the street from our apartment building on the corner stood a crumbling, abandoned building with boarded-up windows, graffiti, and overgrown bushes and grass. As a child, it was the definition of what a haunted house looked like, and I never walked past it. I later learned this was New Brighton Village Hall, which provided an important space for the community.

James Whitford, in the French Second Empire style, designed an impressive architectural structure, completed one hundred years before I was born. After completion, it served as the village system of local government and teemed with village offices and institutions, such as the Staten Island Institute of Arts and Sciences. It also served the community as a police station and a court and offered youth activities and a health clinic. The building was designated a historic landmark by the New York City Landmarks Preservation Commission in 1965.

After a fire in 1969, the hall was abandoned. In October 1971, the city auctioned the building for $26,000 to the Martin Luther King Heritage House, a nonprofit planning to create a community center. Sadly, fundraising stalled and the project was abandoned. In 1985, an out-of-state developer purchased the property with plans to create affordable housing. The following year, Reagan's Tax Reform Act of 1986 was passed, causing major changes to the tax benefits of the project. It failed due to the elimination of tax credits on rental housing. This was the start of the "trickle-down effect" theory of tax cuts and loose regulations for corporations and the wealthy, which was supposed to eventually drip crumbs down to the poor; it never did and still does not. The property passed from one owner to another who promised renovation that never developed. After decades of failed plans to preserve the building, the former village hall was demolished in 2004 after the Department of Buildings deemed it unsafe and a danger.

The impact of federally funded community-based organizations who work toward improving the social, health, and well-being of the area residents can be life-changing, especially for children in insecure environments at home who can benefit from these offerings.

Congress passed a bill the year I was born to create a nationwide system of affordable sliding-scale childcare centers providing day care and after-school care to assist middle- and low-income single-parent families mostly headed by women. It was swiftly vetoed by Richard Nixon, leaving children home in vulnerable positions and without the opportunity for the guidance and mentorship provided by community programs.

From first grade on, I was home alone before and after school. Although it fostered within me a strong sense of independence, creativity, and capability beyond my years, it stemmed from an unhealthy place. There is a fine line between independence and feeling lonely, alone, and isolated.

The existing unmet emotional needs and lack of a bond with my primary caretaker only grew larger and left me with the perception that I could not depend on anyone but myself. Mother was not available, whether she was physically present or not. Being left alone at home without the ability to safely care for myself or protect myself in the face of danger would prove to have serious and lifelong consequences for me. It all started with an unlocked door.

Chapter Two

FALSE PROPHETS
AND RAVENING WOLVES

José de Calasanz was born in Spain in 1557. After being ordained a priest, he later moved to Rome to pursue pastoral missions. One day, while walking through a poor area of the city, he was so moved by the misery of the children who lived there, he claimed to have heard the voice of God, who told him to "give yourself to the poor, teach these children, and care about them." In 1597, he founded an educational system called the Pious Schools, which provided free education to boys from poor families in Rome. The priests, known as Piarists, took four solemn vows: poverty, chastity, obedience, and dedication to educating male children. The schools flourished and expanded into other villages.

By 1629, there were accusations against the Piarists of "impure friendships with schoolboys" and allegations of "impurities" committed by the pious priests. Modern-day Vatican archive researchers uncovered a letter from Calasanz to a school administrator referencing the first accusation: "I want you to know that Your Reverence's sole aim is to cover up this great shame in order that it does not come to the notice of our superiors."

An accused priest was investigated and instead of being

punished was promoted to headmaster and later to inspector. Eventually, he took over Calasanz's position as head of the order. As more abusers were discovered, they, too, were promoted and moved to new schools under the *promoveatur ut amoveatur* or "promotion to remove" method. However, incompetence, over-expansion, and loss of patronage due to the sordid reputations of many priests eventually led to the suppression of the order. The reason given at the time was Calasanz's close association with Galileo, a target of the church who was convicted of heresy in 1633 and became the best-known casualty of the Inquisition. After the suppression, the scandal eventually became public, yet the order was reestablished decades later in the late seventeenth century and went on to have many famous pupils, such as Wolfgang Amadeus Mozart. It still exists today.

Calasanz was canonized in 1767. In 1948, in the ultimate elevation of a man who was complicit in the sexual abuse of children, he was named the universal patron saint of Christian schools. This is irony in its finest definition and, sadly, just one example of an unfathomable number of recorded and unrecorded occurrences and concealments of the sexual abuse of children by clergy who were protected by the church and sent to other unsuspecting and naive communities, creating crisis and lifelong trauma in innocent children.

St. Paul's Catholic School, founded in 1924 as part of the Archdiocese of New York, served the population of New Brighton, a mostly blue-collar community with large families who for decades populated the school. From the 1930s to the 1980s, nearly every member of my family filled the church pews as congregants and school seats as students. I would be the last.

St. Paul, in 1 Corinthians 14:34, stated, "Women should remain silent in the churches. They are not allowed to speak, but must be in submission," which was considered along with 1

Timothy 2:12, "But I suffer not a woman to teach, nor to usurp authority over the man, but to be in silence," as part of the continuous theme of the subservience of women in Catholicism.

My indoctrination into Catholicism at St. Paul's began with the second story of creation. I was taught the well-known tale of Eve, who was fashioned from a rib taken from Adam while he slept. After the notorious apple fiasco, Eve was labeled an untrustworthy sinner, and Adam was given rule over her. Because of Eve's great sin, women, tasked with the job of childbirth, would forever experience great pain during the birthing process. To sum it up, men cannot trust women and women cannot trust women.

The teachings continued with the story of Mary Magdalene. I was taught she was a prostitute who met Jesus, quickly came to regret her sinful life, apologized, and washed his feet. Through these stories, I was taught what a prostitute was, that women were incapable, incompetent sinners, not to be trusted, and must, for the good of all, be submissive to men. These teachings served to reinforce what I had already learned at home.

Later, I discovered how the theme of the flawed woman originated in the first creation story through the tale of Lilith, the initial first woman. Lilith was created equal to man from the dust of the ground, but upon exerting her equal power and refusing to submit to a dominating Adam, she was cast out of paradise and became a demonic succubus who fed on babies and consorted with Lucifer. I would also learn the true story of Mary Magdalene, who was most likely the companion of Jesus. She was the person who received more teachings than any of the Apostles and played many significant roles. Yet her status and reputation were stolen by the envy of resentful men, who turned her into merely a repentant whore. Instead of being revered, she was slandered, degraded, and silenced.

One of the most important things I learned is that if a lie is repeated enough, it becomes truth.

Mother left at dawn for work at the nursing home, leaving me to dress and prepare for school on my own. On most days, I walked to school with my neighbor, but on some I would walk by myself, trailing behind a neighborhood mom walking her child to school. I had a key on a piece of yarn I wore around my neck, tucked underneath my school uniform, to lock the apartment door in the morning and to let myself in when I returned.

On some days, as I left the apartment building to walk to school, our upstairs neighbor would catch me going out the door and tell me to go back in and brush my hair, which I usually forgot to do. She, her husband, and two daughters younger than me moved in after my family left. I usually forgot to perform basic grooming tasks like washing my face or brushing my hair or my teeth. Grooming and cleanliness were not strong points, as I was not taught to master them. When I bathed, it was quickly done, because of a deep fear of water. Mother told me my fear of water came from seeing the movie *Jaws* when it was released in 1975 when I was four years old. She told me how a group of family members went to see it and took me with them. I did not remember seeing the movie but thought it must be true; why else was I absolutely terrified to take a bath? I did remember how I once loved being in the pool with my older cousins before it was taken down and they all moved away.

After school, I would watch television, sitting cross-legged on a kitchen chair in the center of the living room so that my feet did not touch the carpet. Our apartment building had a rodent and insect problem, and it was a daily stress. The mice usually stayed underneath the couch, but sometimes when I sat on the chair quietly watching television, they scurried and raced across the rug to the chair on the other side of the room. Sometimes I would stand on the chair with a heavy encyclopedia and wait for one to run across the room. As soon as it darted across, I would try to time the dropping of the heavy book to crush it. I never crushed one. They were too fast. Other methods for keeping them in their hiding places included tapping on the encyclopedia to make sounds alerting them to my presence or stomping with heavy feet as I made my way around the apartment. I wore my shoes all the time, except when I was sleeping. My only hope was that they slept at night too, although I imagined them crawling on me or burrowing through my clothing while I slept. I worried I would open my bag at school and one would pop out.

At night, the couch became the bed I shared with Mother until I was about eight years old and received hand-me-down furniture from an older cousin—a full bedroom set just for me, with a bed, dresser, and even a small nightstand. It was white with gold trim. I thought the furniture brightened up our otherwise-drab apartment.

The problem with pests did not end with mice. In the kitchen, there were water bugs the size of my small hand. I have never seen such large bugs before or since. Mother kept the outer portion of the gas-stove cooking area wrapped with tinfoil, and at night, when they came out, I heard them crawling on it, their legs marching on the foil as they looked for their nightly meal. Sometimes one came out during the day, but the nighttime was when they freely roamed and when I would not enter the kitchen. I must have only slept out of pure exhaustion.

These memories are clear and etched in my mind as are the rare visits with Father.

On one occasion, he took me to a store to get a coat for winter. I had just started second grade. It was 1978 and the movie *Grease* had been released over the summer. I do not remember who took me to the movies to see it, but I loved it—the music, the singing, the dancing, and especially Olivia Newton-John. I convinced Father to buy me a leather motorcycle jacket like the greasers wore and just like the one Sandy wears at the end of the movie when she has her big transformation. It was a little big, but it was my dream come true. I was able to wear it to school once before it was taken back to the store and returned for a proper, warm, wool coat.

I only saw him once or twice after that. Once the sporadic visits stopped completely, I worked hard to remember his face, holding the image in my mind; I did not want to forget him.

Several times during my years at St. Paul's, the school would put out a warning of a random predator who was driving around the area trying to pick up kids, usually in a van. The one I remember most was the man in the green van. Instead of walking to school during those times, I would run all the way, looking out for him as I raced along. One morning, while running, I turned onto the long street that led to the school when out of nowhere a big German shepherd with a black face charged at me from the side and clasped his jaws onto my right forearm.

The dog gnawed at my arm through my coat, tearing the wool sleeve and angrily swinging his head back and forth, tossing and tugging me, his saliva soaking into my coat. I thought the man in the green van would surely catch me now, thanks to this stupid dog. Because it was cold, I was wearing my proper, warm, wool coat. If it were summer, he would have bitten right through my arm. I quietly begged him to let go. I did not scream or panic. I just quietly begged the dog to let go of me. I counted to ten repetitively, hoping each time I landed on ten it would end. Finally, I heard yelling; a man raced toward me, shouting at the dog. I had never seen the man before. What if it was him? As soon as the dog let go, I turned and ran the rest of the way to school.

That dog was a metaphor for what was to come into my life and what had already been there without my knowing—someone or something coming out of nowhere to attack me, grip me, and hold me down while I was too small and not strong enough to escape. The process of counting to ten until I was freed was eerily familiar to me. I had to walk the same route the next day and each day thereafter alone. My danger watch list was growing.

During this same school year, the first of two life-changing traumas occurred. I was home alone after school, engrossed in my usual work of trying to kill mice while watching television from my post in the middle of the room, when the unlocked apartment door opened and a group of teenage boys came in. They were laughing loudly and piled into the living room where I sat. I only recognized one, the brother of my upstairs neighbor. His sister-in-law was supposed to watch out for me while Mother was at work, so I thought maybe he was looking out for me today. After a few seconds, he told them all to leave. He followed them to the door and shut and locked it. As he turned the corner and came back into the living room, he slowly walked to each window and pulled the shades down one by one. As he arrived at the fourth and final one, he turned to me and said, "We are finally alone."

He told me to sit on the couch. I froze. I never sat on the couch. However, I submissively stood, went to the couch, and sat close to the corner. I held the heavy encyclopedia in my lap. He grabbed the book and put it on the floor, kneeling in front of me. He removed my pants and underwear and put his mouth on my private area. I left my body almost immediately and floated up to the ceiling. I was looking down at what was happening and wondered why he was doing this. I was immobilized with fear. I do not remember how long this went on or what happened afterward. I do not remember if he threatened to hurt me if I told anyone or if he simply left. I could not hear nor could I feel my body. I remained seated on the couch for a long while. I never said a word to anyone, and going forward, when I was home alone, I made certain the door was locked and positioned a chair under the doorknob so no one could enter without me moving it first.

Each day when Mother returned from work, she had to knock, and I moved the chair and opened the door. She never asked why. I never told. I never saw him again.

The laughter of the group of boys combined with the four words he uttered, "We are finally alone," echoed throughout my life. The disturbing memory of his actions haunted me. Each time it arose, I stuffed it down deeper and deeper. The memory gradually stretched from the perspective of a child to that of a woman. It remained a well-preserved source of fear that an unpredictable assault, like the dog attack in definition only, could happen at any moment. Still, it took thirty-six years for me to reveal the truth and speak the words aloud: "I was molested by a relative of my neighbor who lived upstairs on the second floor." Writing these words causes my heart to beat faster. Many of my early life memories are blurry but have been becoming clearer through this writing and research. This was one of a few memories that remained permanently clear as day.

In the summer of 1981, my danger watch list grew again to include the fear of being kidnapped and murdered. A young girl named Molly, seven years old, was sent to the corner store in her neighborhood just a few miles from ours and never seen again. Gone without a trace. Her photo appeared in the newspaper under the word "Missing" in giant letters, and a reward was offered for information. This period also brought the era of placing photos of missing children on the backs of milk cartons. Many mornings, I stared at Molly's face and the faces of other missing children while I ate my cereal. I heard the killer was an escaped mental patient who snatched children off the street and murdered them. He may have had a hook for a hand and was a real-life boogeyman.

The eight years I spent at St. Paul's were extremely traumatic. Physical, psychological, and emotional abuse were just as present as learning the ABCs. The priests and nuns, under the pretense of religious teachings, used images of hell and torturous punishments as potential results of even the slightest rule violations by us juvenile sinners. Thankfully, God was forgiving, and during the weekly allotted time in the confessional booth, we were given the opportunity to confess our sins to the priests, who would prescribe the number of prayers needed for them to be pardoned. Reciting three Hail Marys and five Our Fathers was what saved us from the week's offenses. I would have gladly said a hundred of each just to get out of that dark box.

Physical contact in the form of a smack across the cheek or on the back of the hand was always a whisper away. Sister Mary Darcy, the school principal, would turn her large, pointy crucifix ring around to line it up with her palm so when she smacked the area, it would hurt more and, if hard enough or done in precise repetition, would leave a small imprint of the cross on your skin. She reigned over us with an iron fist and put the fear of her and God into us. She taught us our emotions did not matter and we should be silent, be obedient, and conform to their rigid standards without question.

Sister Mary Darcy was a small woman, thin and frail, who relished power and control. She physically abused the boys more than the girls, but everyone had a smack at some point, and no one was spared from her screaming in your face. The students she picked on the most would eventually grow tired of the constant physical abuse and dare to talk back. They were swiftly taken out of the room, often returning with the small imprint of a cross on their reddened cheek and held-back tears in their eyes.

From my earliest years in the school, it became routine for Sister Mary Darcy to call me to the office to tell me Mother was late with paying my tuition and that unless I returned to school the next day with a check, I would not be allowed in. Several times she appeared at the classroom door and combined it with other announcements to the teacher and the entire class. No one ever made fun of me or teased me about it. We were a small class and grew to be a close-knit group of friends. Socially bonded through shared trauma with a sense of empathy and emotional support for one another, we remained sympathetic to the punishments and forced humiliations of Sister Mary Darcy. Despite the unpleasantness, these types of shared experiences bonded our group together in solidarity.

We spent eight years of our young lives through an important growth period under stressful circumstances, which formed a lifelong camaraderie. Whether we remain in each other's lives decades later or not, we remain bonded. I had several kind friends at school, and I was embraced by them and their families, who made a difference in my young life. They were my resilience points and what gave me cherished moments of freedom and friendship.

Aside from Sister Mary Darcy, there were only two other nuns who taught in the school during my time there, one of whom was Sister Mary Dolores, a large woman who resembled a Weeble, the popular egg-shaped roly-poly toy. Sister Mary Dolores was the Hardy to Sister Mary Darcy's Laurel. The Costello to the Abbott. A classically and comedically paired fat-and-skinny duo. She kept a thick wooden paddle on her desk to use as a punishment tool. The infliction of pain from her paddle ranged between light taps for unruly handwriting and a broken hand. Only the brave challenged her for fear of worse. She and Sister Mary Darcy were members of the Sisters of the Presentation of the Blessed Virgin Mary, a Roman Catholic religious congregation, founded in Ireland in 1775 and brought to Staten Island in 1884. In keeping with their vows, did they each lead a contemplative life of prayer in private? Did the Sisters ask for God's forgiveness for their cruel and heartless behavior, or did they enjoy their callous power over defenseless children? Perhaps their shameful actions were related to the lack of actual power they had as women within their church.

By sixth grade, girls were eligible to try out for the cheerleading squad. My class was not large, and almost every girl in the class came to the gym for cheerleading tryouts. We all made the team, and I was voted by the group to be captain. I could not believe it. I did not ask or volunteer, it was just a part of the process, and when the group was asked, I was picked. The feeling of acceptance fed my deep desire to be included and to be seen as someone whom others would put their trust in.

Soon after, we all reported to the gym for our first practice as a team. I did not know what being captain meant but thought I would, at the least, get to stand in the front next to the coach. I even brushed my hair before leaving for school that morning. We gathered in the center of the gym, but just before starting, Sister Mary Darcy appeared at the side door. She entered and walked across the shiny gym floor, her thick, clicking heels echoing like thunder. Her presence held the air of dark clouds suffocating a bright, sunny day. She walked straight toward me and asked for me to follow her into the entrance to the girls' bathroom. She opened the door and motioned for me to go through. I entered and we stood in the small area at the bottom of the stairs, which led to the bathroom. I had assumed this would be about my unpaid tuition again, but this time was different. She said she had something important to tell me.

She explained how another girl, who was a year older and in the seventh grade, was sure the team had made a mistake when they picked me to be the captain. She was sure they had meant to pick her. Sister Mary Darcy went on to explain it was all just a misunderstanding. The other girl was older and more deserving of the title of captain because she came from a good family who gave money to the school and church, and it would just be better if I stepped aside and let her take the role. I was crushed, and I believed her. Why would they pick me? Of course, it was a mistake. Why would anyone think I was important enough to be captain?

As we exited and went back into the gymnasium, she noted my tuition was late again and told me to remind Mother I would not be able to come back to school if it was not paid right away. The tears filling my eyes quickly retracted on my walk back to the group gathered in the middle of the gym, and I rejoined as if nothing had happened. Now there was a skill I was good at. And there she was, the other girl who was from a good family who gave money to the school and church and paid her tuition on time, standing next to the coach, ready to assume her role as captain. She looked at me and smiled. I was sure she was used to getting what she wanted, just as much as I was used to the exact opposite. Things carried on as if nothing had happened, and no one said a word about it, including me.

I did not continue long with cheering. Besides what happened, I only remember Mother yelling about having to spend money on the uniform and saddle shoes I ended up not using. Standing on the sidelines and cheering on the boys was not what I wanted to be doing anyway. I liked sports and was more interested in playing softball and basketball. Thanks to my friend May and her family, who were neighbors, I was able to play. May's mom took me with them to every practice and game; otherwise, I would not have been able to get there. I must have played in a hundred games; Mother attended none.

I spent a lot of time with May's family at their home. They were an important source of resilience for me. They had a pool and a basketball net, and we spent hours swimming, playing, listening to music, and watching movies. Although I would never be entirely comfortable, they helped me be less afraid of being in water. But I learned to love swimming and thought how ridiculous I had been when I was younger, holding the fear of a shark being in a pool or any body of water anywhere at any time, ready to pop up and eat me. We watched the movie *The Outsiders* again and again, crying at the end when Johnny died and again when Darrel died. We read the book, written by S. E. Hinton, passing it back and forth repeatedly. None of us knew S. E. Hinton was a woman or that she wrote the book when she was just sixteen years old. Like many female authors throughout history, she was advised to use her initials so the book would not be dismissed solely due to her gender. The Robert Frost poem referenced in the story, "Nothing Gold Can Stay," touched me deeply. This was when I found my love of stories and poetry. Books taught me how to dream and sparked my imagination of being a writer, performer, and storyteller. I would transcribe the poem repeatedly and try to understand the meaning of each line and why it made me feel the way it did. I thought it was beautiful:

> *Nature's first green is gold,*
> *Her hardest hue to hold.*
> *Her early leaf's a flower;*
> *But only so an hour.*
> *Then leaf subsides to leaf.*
> *So Eden sank to grief,*
> *So dawn goes down to day.*
> *Nothing gold can stay.*[1]

My interpretation of the poem was nothing good lasts. There was grief, pain, and loss in life and . . . nothing gold could stay. It's a great life if you don't weaken.

Around this time, the school offered a music program led by Father Comghan, who'd previously served at St. Paul's but had been moved to another parish soon after I first entered the school.

He was a celebrated Irish musician and played the concertina and flute. The program offered interested students the chance to learn an instrument. I chose guitar and was even able to bring it home on the weekends. I'd put on the radio or a record and spend hours trying to play along. Without explanation, the program was short-lived, and I had to return the borrowed guitar after just a few lessons. Although brief, it served as my introduction to guitar and sparked my love for the instrument.

In 2018, during my research into allegations of sexual abuse against priests who spent time at St. Paul's, I read an article in *Catholic New York*, the official newspaper of the Archdiocese of New York, and learned the probable cause behind the fleeting music program. Promoted to monsignor in 2006, Father Comghan had several allegations of sexual abuse filed against him. The allegations were found credible and substantiated. He was assigned to St. Paul's from 1969 to 1976 before he was transferred to another parish on Staten Island. Several years later, he was transferred again to a parish in Brooklyn. He was defrocked in 2018.

Soon after the music program ended, Sister Mary Darcy stopped me in the hallway and told me I would be helping with some cleaning in the rectory on Saturday. Because Mother worked most Saturdays, this gave me something productive to do. I thought it was because my tuition was late again, as usual, and maybe this was a way to make up for it.

On Saturday, Mother walked me the few blocks to the rectory, which stood at the back of the school, on her way to work, two blocks north. I would spend the day there and be picked up on her way home. The entrance was on the side of the house behind the auditorium. I walked up the wooden steps and knocked lightly on the screen door. After just a moment, Father Logue opened the door and motioned for me to enter. He stepped out and had a few words with Mother. I waited at the entrance. This was my first time in the rectory. It smelled like mothballs. A drink and some cookies were on the table.

I heard a noise in the next room. Father Diarmada stepped into the kitchen. He wore a long necklace with a large gold crucifix that hung at his stomach. As he began to speak, as he often did, he held the top part of the chain, allowing the large cross affixed with the dying Jesus to sway back and forth like a hypnotizing tool.

"Kathleen is here to help us today, Father, isn't that nice?" Father Logue said. "She is just having a snack before we get started."

I sat at the table and watched the door, waiting for other kids to show up.

"Have you seen the movie *Blue Lagoon*, Kathleen? You look like the star of the movie, Brooke Shields. She is such a beautiful girl."

This was not the first time Father Logue told me I looked like Brooke Shields. I thought priests were not allowed to look at girls that way.

After I finished a few cookies and some sips of apple juice, Father Logue brought me into another room. He told me to sit and wait for him to return. There was a small couch and several wooden chairs arranged around a coffee table with a bible in the center. There was no television. Several crucifixes of varying sizes adorned the walls. I sat on one of the chairs and noticed how even though it was daytime, the room was slightly dark from the closed curtains, and I could barely see. I started to feel scared.

The door opened and the rest of my time there is in disorganized memory—pain, the darkness of the room, the necklace, and the smell of mothballs. My clearest memory of the day is standing at the screen door waiting for Mother to pick me up, my body shaking and throbbing with pain as I stared through the screen at the back of the school building at the large gold cross that hung in the corner.

First, in gentle whispers, I asked God why he let this happen to me and softly prayed for help. My prayers quickly evolved into harshly cursing the God who let this happen to me. It was the exact moment of the hardening of my heart, sealing within it a rage that consumed my world for a long time. And in my mind, a continuance of fragmented memory of what occurred and what followed persisted: the walk home, vomiting on the sidewalk, lying on my bed, crying into my pillow for what seemed like forever, and Mother throwing my clothes in the garbage, including my cherished Jordache jeans I had begged for and received as a present for Christmas.

Exhausted from utter shock, physical pain, and intermittent hysterical crying, I was left in a sleepy, dreamlike daze, where I thought it was all just a nightmare. It grew dark outside. I was in and out of sleep when my aunt entered the room and sat beside me on my bed. She softly stroked my face and hair. I appreciated her tenderness. This type of affection was something Mother would never have offered. She spoke softly and told me things would be all right if I could just forget. She pointed to a wooden jewelry box she left for me on my dresser. *Just forget.*

The next morning, I reached for the jewelry box. I held it in my hands. It had painted silk doors with fancily dressed women paused in dance on each side. Behind the doors were three drawers, and when the bottom one was pulled out it played the melody to "Fly Me to the Moon." I imagined the women happily twirling to the melody, their long satin and lace-covered dresses floating just above the ground in a wavy slow motion, as they smiled and danced, their hands reaching out for one another.

Many memories of the short-lived aftermath persisted along with the wooden jewelry box, which remains in my possession as a piece of macabre memorabilia. By the following evening, Mother and my aunt sat together in front of me and spoke the words told to them by The Priests.

"You don't want to hurt a man's reputation, especially a holy man," Mother said. Instead of demanding justice, she chose to protect The Priests instead of me. "Sometimes bad things happen, but you must forget about it. Just do not think about it, and it will go away."

Mother had routinely taught me the code of silence and the important skill of self-induced amnesia: when bad things happen, just bury them as deep as you can until you forget. Our family passed down this code like other families passed on cherished recipes from generation to generation. I learned to be a victim of circumstance who wore the guise of normalcy the best I could. I was trained to believe there was no option for legitimate justice. What was a woman to do but shut up and move on?

Soon after, my aunt took me with her family to Disney World to help me forget. A valiant effort. I had never been on a plane or farther away than the Poconos or the Jersey Shore, one time each. I have limited memory of the trip but recall certain things like listening to "Cum on Feel the Noize" by Quiet Riot on the plane repeatedly. At a show in the theme park, I was picked by the host in a group-theater setting and had to stand up and say my name and where I was from: "Kathleen Rose Morgan, from New York." One night, after a disagreement between my aunt and cousin, I heard my aunt's words: "We brought Kathleen here for her to have a nice time, not to listen to us argue. She hears enough arguing at home. All she hears is yelling!" It was the first time someone acknowledged what it was usually like in my home, and I was grateful to know someone had noticed.

It was nice to be away, but I was deep in pain and rage and the only feeling I took home with me was a hatred of Disney characters, especially the princesses. I must have been the only young girl there who wanted to punch them in the face, not wear a crown and take a photo.

As I write this, I think about the Disney marketing campaigns with sports stars yelling into the camera after winning a big game, "I'm going to Disney World!" The satire is astounding.

What happened to me was never spoken of again. The rage, which had permeated me during the trip, erupted in self-destructive ways. I cut at my wrists with the point of a sharp steak knife while I took baths. I made small nicks and scratches, just deep enough to bleed a little bit so I could watch the small drops of blood sink into the water and dissolve. This relieved some of the otherwise-unyielding pain I was feeling inside. Death by a thousand cuts. I am sure there were visible signs, but no one noticed. During basketball games at school, I charged at full speed toward an opposing team member and sent her flying across the gym floor. I became severely aggressive, an obscured cry out for help, but no one seemed to notice, or if they did, it was buried and no action was taken, likely because of the fear of me speaking the truth. I was left to plummet.

Being kept in the place where the abuse occurred resulted in living in a constant state of fear that it would happen again. Smothered and profoundly betrayed, even if I found the courage to come forward, I was convinced no one would believe me. I was a small fish in their big pond, and they were at the top of the food chain. I avoided The Priests and mastered the skill of dissociation. Not long after, Father Logue was gone. There is no mention of him in the history of the school. He was simply erased. Father Diarmada remained. And I was never asked for late tuition money again.

My rape was swept under the mountainous rug of the Catholic Church, a crowded terrain teeming with secrets and the lost innocence of broken children at the hands of the false prophets who wore the robes of God as sheep's clothing.

They are the ravening wolves who lay in wait behind their cassocks and collars until the moment arrives when they pounce with sharp fangs and slippery claws to tear the bodies of their prey limb from limb.

At school and at home, I had been forcefully instructed never to speak about what happened or there would be consequences . . . and reminded, even if I did tell, that no one would ever believe me. In keeping with our school's namesake, I had been taught to see myself as inferior, a preteen seductive temptress culpable for sin, responsible for holding up the reputation of repulsive men, and excluded from justice. I had been degraded and silenced and bore the weight of the disgraceful shame of an indefensible crime committed by The Perpetrators, including Mother, who saw me as a disposable object. It was the seizing of whatever was left of me after the first molestation and was the beginning of my firm and absolute hatred of God, religion, myself, Disney characters, and the song "Fly Me to the Moon."

"You don't want to hurt a man's reputation, especially a holy man" joined the other reprehensible words etched into my bones: "We are finally alone." The power of these haunting words kept me from completely forgetting.

By the time I started eighth grade, with my secrets safely tucked away, I began smoking cigarettes on a regular basis. At the top of our street was a soda shop called Mac's, where Mother sent me to buy cigarettes and Coke syrup from the soda fountain for my frequently upset stomach. She never seemed to notice any cigarettes missing from the pack or the smell of lingering bits of smoke when she arrived home from work.

In spring, I tried cannabis for the first time. Annalyn, a friend from school, took it from her mother and we smoked it on the way to the local Little League fields to watch classmates play baseball. I was already an experienced cigarette smoker and took a few puffs. It made me feel like someone else, carefree, and immensely better. It gave an impression of gliding just above the ground and the shitstorm of my life. Some might see Anna-lyn's procurement of cannabis as a bad thing, but it was quite the opposite. From that moment on, it became my survival tool and medicine for the next two decades.

On weekends, I traveled on the bus to the Staten Island Mall or the adjacent movie theater with friends. I brought enough of my collected cigarettes for everyone, and we sat in the back row of the theater, smoked, and watched movies. At twelve years old, we purchased tickets for any movie no matter the rating and were never admonished by anyone for smoking. The area was across from the landfill, and as we approached, the smell of rotting garbage permeated the bus. Upon exiting, we pulled our shirts over our mouths to breathe. The smell was overwhelming and noxious year-round, but it was especially unbearable in the summer months.

The area, called Fresh Kills, had been purchased by the city in 1946 for use as a temporary landfill in exchange for developmental resources and other forms of support for the island. It was considered worthless swampland, and, by 1948, over two thousand acres of land became the depository for the city's trash. The landfill grew increasingly toxic and environmentally destructive and by 1955 had grown to be the world's largest landfill. Millions of tons of malodourous decomposing trash and unregulated medical waste were dumped. Feral dog packs and rats roamed freely. Rat poison was added to the piles of waste but had no effect. Instead, predatory birds were brought into this festering wasteland, and it was preposterously declared a wild-bird sanctuary. Before the Fresh Kills Landfill was born, the area was an actual sanctuary. Far from being worthless swampland, it was filled with thriving tidal wetlands, forests, and fauna and had a robust native plant, animal, and bird ecosystem.

The surrounding area included a mix of homes, schools, and retail businesses filled with residents who ingested the methane gas bonded with organic compounds released into the air for miles. Staten Island traditionally had and continues to have the worst rates of birth defects, cancer, asthma, and other medical issues within the five boroughs of New York City.

After fifty-three years of operation, this temporary landfill closed on March 22, 2001, only to be opened again just under five months later to receive the remains from the World Trade Center site. The landfill became a forensic sorting area. Workers carefully sifted through over one million tons of debris for over one million hours. Behind them, with the view of the cityscape of lower Manhattan missing the World Trade Center towers, workers recovered more than four thousand human remains, but sadly only three hundred people were identified. Sixteen hundred personal effects were found, and the remaining debris was buried. A memorial added to the site in 2011 honors the victims.

Impermeable-cover capping of the mounds started in the late 1990s. Construction began on Freshkills Park in 2008 and is scheduled for completion in 2037. Today, the park is a symbol of renewal with open grasslands, waterways, and public spaces. It will be the largest park in New York City when it is completed.

After graduating from St. Paul's, I sank further into a quicksand of grief and installed an impermeable cover over the life-altering experiences I was subjected to at home and at school. Once I was out from under their clutches, it was as if I were shot out of a rocket into real life, completely unprepared, traumatized, and alone. I immediately became defiant and reckless. No plans, no direction or vision for the future, quietly simmering in a hidden toxic anger, frozen in moments of trauma. Merely making it through each day was a challenge. Within one year, I was a recurring runaway, a high school dropout, and a drug addict who understood the meaning of the poem. I had been gold but was now the dying leaf, clinging to the rotted roots of a diseased tree watching the dawn go down. The branches too weak to hold me, I plunged to the ground to decay in dreary grief amid the betrayal of the light.

Nothing gold can stay.

Chapter Three

THE OBSCENE WEIGHT OF SUICIDAL THOUGHT AND SELF-DESTRUCTION

The dysfunction and trauma I experienced as a young child, coupled with Mother colluding with the offenders to cover the abuse, instilled in me strong feelings of shame and an unrelenting feeling of being unsafe. The Priests who committed the most heinous crime against me were not held accountable, and I was coerced to quietly carry the oppressive weight of their illicit and sickening actions and secrets.

I entered my teenage years in a deep state of unconsciousness and delusion. The summer following my graduation from St. Paul's, I promptly fell off the edge of a cliff into a raging river of wrong crowds, drugs, alcohol, and self-damaging bad choices. With no life preserver, I quickly sank into a whirlwind of oblivion. My trauma-induced world became a full-time job of forgetting and pointless risk. I did not know who I was or who I was supposed to be and had no guidance on how to navigate the world outside the prison bars of Catholic school and the stark quiet of my home. While I was physically freed from their custody, I was not free mentally or emotionally. I raised a white flag of surrender and buried everything so deep within me, it would never surface again. They had won.

All I wanted was to be normal. I was obsessed with the desire and longing to be loved and cared for, and because of this, I was lured into situations that were not in my best interest simply because I was being paid attention to, even if the attention was ill intended. Bitter and vengeful, the more trouble I found myself in, the more I dug in even deeper. I was never offered a lifeline, only degradation and blame for my many missteps. Mother, surely worried I might tell the truth of what had happened, sat back and watched me self-destruct. She relished in the resulting attention she received as a hard-working single mother with an out-of-control daughter. Perversely, it satisfied her otherwise-unmet need for respect and regard.

What should have been my advancement into my teenage years of high school and exploring life became a roller coaster of suicidal thoughts and self-destruction. I was smart, and even through the traumas in elementary school, I always achieved good grades. I should have been stepping on the path to success, but as soon as I set foot into the doorway of my short-lived high school career, I plunged into a swift downward spiral. I had already dipped my toes into drugs and alcohol, but after just a few months into ninth grade, I was using every day.

According to a recently obtained transcript, I was absent eighty-five days during my first year. I acquired street smarts instead of school smarts. In the corner bodega, I bought loosies for a quarter and forty-ounce beers with my lunch money. For years, I had been out of my body, but drinking and smoking took me out of my head, which was a relief. It became my flight response. Several times, while cutting out of school, I was picked up by police patrols and transported back to school, only to walk out the back door.

Toward the end of my disastrous freshman year, a school advisor set up an appointment for me to see a counselor. I reluctantly showed up at the office one block away from the school and was greeted by a woman. We stepped into an office and sat across from each other. I immediately delivered lame excuses about my absences.

When I finished talking, she said, "Hello, Kathleen, you don't remember me? I am Jill's mother."

Everything faded. I did not hear another word she said, although I did see her lips moving. My mind took me back to grammar school. Jill had been a classmate. I had gone to their home with other friends for sleepovers. The house was big and beautiful, with a swing set in the backyard, next to a big park. I sensed my body swinging back and forth, laughing with my sweet, normal friends. The woman I was now staring at prepared freshly baked cookies and brought them out to a nicely set table in the yard. I remembered learning Jill was adopted and thinking she was the luckiest girl in the world. Her new parents must have rescued her from terrible ones and now she had a good life.

Back in the room with Jill's mother, my eyes flooded with tears as I responded, "I'm sorry, I do not remember you." The truth was I remembered every minute detail of the times I visited her home. This moment could have been a lifeline for me if I had told her the truth about what had happened. She may have helped lift me out of the mess I could not find my way out of. Instead, I stood and hurriedly left without saying a word, drenched in shame at what I'd turned out to be. I never saw her again.

My sophomore year was even more of a blur, validated by my transcript, which states my absences as 112 days, even though I do not remember being there at all. I was unrecognizable. Any bit of myself remained buried under piles of trauma. I was locked into complete failure. It became harder and harder to make it through each day. I had been silenced, blamed, and shamed by the one person who was responsible for my well-being as a child. Mother made me believe it was all my fault. Something was wrong with me. The worst part was that I'd started to believe her.

It was the mid-1980s and the crack epidemic had taken hold. It was only a matter of time before I tried it and became addicted. Crack exploded into widespread use because of the intense euphoric result it produced when smoked.

It takes only eight seconds for the effect to reach the brain, releasing a large amount of dopamine. The high only lasts around ten minutes, and as it dissipates, the dopamine plummets. In the span of a few minutes, one went from an exhilarating high to a depressing and miserable low, producing a deeply addictive result.

The crack epidemic was not viewed with today's relatively compassionate approach toward victims of the opioid scourge. It affected minority and poor communities whose unfortunate residents were not seen as victims of a powerful drug. People were scooped up and put in jail for drug crimes. There were substantial amounts of money to be made in this business, and the crowd I hung out with had several dealers who kept the group readily supplied. As a seller and as a user, it was easy to fall under the spell of an addictive drug, which was not in a person's best interest but served an immediate purpose. For me, it was simply an escape from intolerable pain.

There were times I did not come home for days. Mother screamed at me when I finally showed up, but I did it again and again. I did not know if the screaming was a long-awaited form of concern or a result of the fright of me blowing my cover as a member of the "everything-is-fine, nothing-to-see-here family." I was fourteen going on dead.

Once, after being gone for a week with no contact, I showed up at home to change my clothes and get something to eat. I expected Mother to be at work, but she had the day off. As soon as I walked in the door, she came out of nowhere and grabbed me by my hair. She had a pair of scissors in her hand. She wrapped her fist around my long hair and started cutting and chopping at it. She cut it up to my neck in uneven lengths and smacked me several times in the face while calling me a worthless piece of shit. As soon as she let go, I stared at her for a second, turned around, and walked out the door without saying anything.

Several days later, I arrived home again purely out of necessity. I was strung out, tired, and hungry, and I arrived to the usual degrading taunts.

"Look at you. You look disgusting. What is wrong with you? You are filthy and a little pig, and you only think about yourself. Why are you doing this to me? Aren't you ashamed of yourself? Well, you should be."

I said nothing and slowly walked to the bathroom, just a few steps away, and shut the door. Without any preconceived notion or planning, I opened the medicine cabinet and grabbed a random bottle of prescription pills. Without looking at what they were, I opened the top and put a few at a time into my mouth, turned on the faucet, leaned down, filled my mouth with water, and swallowed. I did this until the bottle was empty. I put the empty bottle in my pocket.

Mother was, as usual, talking to herself in the next room. She continued her usual self-chatter in a whispered voice about what a loser I was. She repeated the word "disgusting" and said she could not deal with me anymore . . . that it was too bad my father did not care about me because he could have taken me.

As I stood at the sink, I stared at the bathtub and flashed to a scene in my mind one year prior, of cutting at my wrist with a steak knife. I wished I'd been brave enough to cut all the way through, but the pills would be a less painful way. I opened the door and walked the few steps across the small living room, past Mother, who still whispered, smoked, and stared at the television. She quieted her voice a bit and mumbled more cruel words under her breath as I walked by and entered my bedroom. I shut the door, removed my shoes, lay on the bed, and whispered, "Goodbye."

Surprisingly, I woke the next morning with a massive, throbbing headache and stomach cramps that led to frequent vomiting. I had never been so tired and could barely stand up. Throughout the day, I hoped each time I fell asleep I did not wake up.

After two days, I gradually improved, but over this time, the sadness at the full realization of my actions was overwhelming. I was alive but I did not know why. I was not happy to be alive, and the feeling became bone-chillingly sad.

Perhaps seeing me so sick stirred a momentary maternal instinct in Mother, who gave a half-assed apology for cutting my hair and hitting me and said she did not know what else to do. I could have thought of many other things, like holding The Priests accountable for what they did to me, instead of making me think I was a damaged, at-fault person, or acknowledging the truth of what happened instead of ignoring it. Although insufficient, it was the first time any apology under any circumstance was given to me, which brought the slightest feeling of gratification. The horrendous incidents that brought me to this place of desperation were never discussed or addressed. It was as if nothing happened.

I had made a serious attempt to take my life, and it scared me. I might try again and succeed. There were many times, because of drugs or the risky situations I found myself in, I wished someone did it for me.

One year later, a lifeline was offered, and I agreed to spend time away for a few weeks in another state with a relative. No one knew about my suicide attempt. Mother never noticed a full bottle of prescription pills was gone. During the few weeks I was away, I spent a great deal of time alone and had plenty of space to think uninterrupted. Without the drugs clouding my mind,

I had a chance to be reflective. I realized there were only two options: live or die. I was fifteen, and it became clear it was up to me to pull myself out of the deep hole I was in. If I was going to live, now was the time to figure out how. Because I hated who I was and the events I was forced to reconcile, I pretended to be someone else. I put on a mask that fit so tightly around my face, I could barely breathe.

When I returned home, I did not go back to high school, as I was already so far behind. After two years, I only had one credit. But I did not go back to the hard drugs and the people who shared them with me either. I hung out with a group of known neighborhood friends who were a step up from where I was before but also not entirely in my best interest. I did not know how to make good choices in any relationships. I had a high tolerance for poor treatment and no healthy boundaries. A childhood tarnished with adverse events stripped away self-esteem and self-worth. If someone was too nice, I did not trust them.

I spent most of my time on the neighborhood streets. On each corner of the entrance to our dead-end street were pubs, one a half block south and the other a half block north. The drinking age was fifteen at the former, or at least it was the first time I was served. The building was constructed in the early 1800s as a three-story structure that had a bar on the first floor and a brothel on the third floor. After a fire, the third floor was lost, but the rest of the building was saved. Tall hedges surrounded the corner property. On occasion, there was a human-sized hole in the otherwise neatly trimmed hedge that someone too drunk to continue standing fell into while waiting for the bus or a taxi.

Inside, the bar was dimly lit and smelled like mothballs, wood polish, and stale beer. The gloomy lighting and the smell of mothballs often brought me back to the rectory, but after two or three drinks, the feeling faded. The bartender said I reminded him of a young lady named Shirley whom he'd dated back when he was a much younger man. He leaned over the intricately carved and polished wooden bar top, his bar rag hanging over his shoulder, and asked, "Hey, Shirley, what can I get for you?"

He never questioned how old I was, nor did anyone else, and he never charged me for a drink. I never went to the other bar; no one did. I had a brief memory of being there as a small child for a Christmas party and sitting on Santa's lap. It was not open regularly and eventually was demolished. It became another empty lot with overgrown weeds and a robust population of rats.

The mask I now wore fit me so well I forgot it was there. In my quest to be normal, I chose to believe wholeheartedly how everything that had occurred since I left St. Paul's was my fault. I could have made better choices when I entered high school. I was broken. Going forward, when painful memories surfaced, I buried them as far as I could and pretended those events never happened—just as I was told. I inflicted myself with situational amnesia.

My relationship with Mother never improved; it was tolerated. She did not love me, and I did not love her, and it was never anything more. I came and went as I pleased with little interaction, not more than an occasional word. Each morning, I put on a fresh, perfectly fitted mask before stepping into the outside world. It tricked everyone who looked at it.

Father died in late spring, a few weeks before my sixteenth birthday. It had been nine years since I had last seen him. He had become a figment of my imagination. I did not remember what he looked like and had no photographs of him. During the darkest of times, I wondered if he might come and help me when things became bad, but he never intervened. I wondered if he knew how my life had progressed since I last saw him. Did he know about my troubles and didn't care like Mother said? I believed her now. He never showed up to prove otherwise.

I hated him, just like I hated her. Before his death, he was hospitalized with cirrhosis and failing organs from a lifetime of alcohol abuse. He knew he was going to die. My sibling was going to see him. When I was told Father asked to see me, I was, as usual, unaided in my trauma-clouded decision-making and said I would not go. However, I asked for a message to be passed on: "Fuck you."

Mother's insults and criticisms quieted as I matured, turning more toward expertly crafted manipulation and familiar lies told recurrently as a form of memory altering, but they never fully went away. I was left to either continue wallowing in my trauma and forfeit my life as she had or claw myself out of the repercussions of my traumatic experiences.

As I realized this, I slowly gained control over some of my erratic behaviors. I started reading books again and listening to music. I walked in a local park and spent time sitting beside a small stream. I revisited all the things I had missed during the last three years of darkness, which had enveloped my life. I spent a lot of time alone. Although I was relieved of constant difficulty and struggles, it would be a few more years before I wielded some power over my life and made better choices. I continued to be entangled with the wrong people. But I obtained my GED, scoring high on each of the test portions, which gave me a boost of confidence I needed.

During this time, I explored Manhattan. Stepping off the ferryboat in the city was like stepping into another world full of possibility. Like a snake shedding its skin, I was able to leave my past behind for a few hours. I walked for miles and learned the subway lines. I was in a place where no one knew me. I was anyone from anywhere.

Shame and fear, combined with manipulated and altered memories, are the components that form an emotional padlock on recollection. They create tightly sutured lips that abusers rely on to keep their victims quiet and shocked into submission. In my case, I was psychologically manipulated to believe that what happened did not happen and if it did happen, I should pretend it didn't. The psychological and emotional stress of this manipulation became embedded in my immature mind. This resulted in the chore of coping with a need for consistent mitigation of an intolerable pain only I recognized as true. I was handed a life sentence of living with the results of the calamitous choices of the adults in the room and a perpetually fleeting consideration of ending my life, even though I overwhelmingly wanted to live.

Chapter Four

THE PRIMAL SCREAM

Science has proven how learning an instrument can alter brain structure,[2] helping with long-term memory, overall development, and alertness. The sensory processes are better integrated through our emotional response to music. Playing an instrument integrates vision, hearing, and touch, creating a change in the structure of the area of the brain called the "corpus callosum." This is the large, C–shaped nerve-fiber bundle located beneath the cerebral cortex. It stretches through the brain and connects the left and right cerebral hemispheres. Its main function is communication between the two, and it plays a key role in cognition. Physical coordination and processing complex and multiple amounts of information require the left and right brain to work together as a team. Using both hands to play an instrument increases the strength of this part of the brain and leads to greater overall multisensory skills. Other ways to strengthen this area would be to use your nondominant hand in place of your dominant one or through exercises like juggling.

Music is an effective, drug-free therapeutic approach and is used as a supportive tool in the treatment of physical and mental challenges.[3] Music therapies are increasingly used as a healing method to aid in various forms of medical treatment. Music helps people cope with stress and activates the body's own capacity to heal. Our bodies automatically adjust to the timing of the music, breathing in and out to match the rhythm, resembling the technique used in therapeutic breathwork practices also used as a healing tool.

The music program I participated in at school in my preteen years was short-lived, and after a few months of lessons, I had to return the borrowed acoustic guitar. Although brief, it introduced me to guitar and the benefits of playing music. During my years of self-obliteration, between twelve and sixteen, everything I found pleasure in completely dropped off my radar, including music. But as I emerged from this period, I rediscovered my love of it. I spent countless hours listening to The Beatles, my early childhood favorite. I escaped into their songs when my older sibling was not home, playing his records on the small turntable I was not supposed to touch. Their songs and voices were avenues to a more colorful and loving world, and I found a sense of peace through them.

I loved all genres of music, but I was heavily drawn to bands like Black Sabbath, Iron Maiden, Slayer, and, my favorite, Metallica. My connection to guitar roared back into my life after hearing their record *Ride the Lightning*, a masterpiece of contrast with soft, beautiful melodies and aggressive, heavily distorted guitar. Listening to this record ignited a spark in my heart and reminded me how much I loved guitar.

My job at a local supermarket was now my way to buy an affordable red Fender Squier guitar from a local music shop. I did not realize I was putting myself on the path that would save my life; I just knew I needed a guitar. I was able to put it on layaway and went weekly to add whatever I could to the balance until it was fully paid.

The day I picked up the guitar was the first step into my new life. When I put the strap over my head and the weight of its body pressed against mine, it felt like a suit of armor shielding me from memorialized trauma and the threat of any potential further damage. I picked out a small amp and a distortion pedal and resumed weekly payments again until the balance was paid. I played every day, sitting for hours, trying to match the notes in my favorite songs. For the first time, I had something to focus on and something healthy to occupy my time and mind.

There were two me's: the one I let people see, and the one I did not. I was still escaping from reality the only way I knew how, by smoking and drinking in excess. I did not always make the best choices about the people I was spending time with, but as I slowly found myself again, my choices improved. Like attracts like. The traumatized, depressed, angry, and fearful side of me attracted people dealing with the same. I came out of a long span of constant negative thoughts and actions, along with the baggage of a traumatized childhood, and attracted negative people and experiences into my life.

Learning to play guitar and becoming enmeshed in music put me on a more positive path. As I redeveloped the compassionate, caring, and loving side of me, I was able to attract the same. My insecurity and shame often were in the way of positive relationships, but I was learning to overcome those feelings while unknowingly reprogramming my brain by playing guitar. But underneath, I was still a phony pretending to be someone else.

The loud, fast, rage-encompassing music I grew to love matched the rage I held in the pit of my stomach, and what came out of my guitar amp was an extension of it. Pleasure, in any form, was not an emotion I was familiar or comfortable with, but I did find it through music. Releasing this rage from my body, via my guitar, helped to soften the anger I held, enough to make it flexible. I spent the next fifteen years releasing the pain and rage embedded within me. It became my fight response. It protected me and sharpened my focus. Incrementally, I released stagnant emotional pain that alleviated some of the tension held in my muscles.

Music calmed my nerves. It also gave me a sense of control that I never had before; I was in charge. Music gave me power, and most importantly, it gave me optimism. I had something to focus on, something to achieve and be proud of, something to take my mind off the truth. It empowered me. Without it, I surely would have not survived.

The musicians I admired also helped to rekindle my love of reading. I read Jim Morrison's poetry and through it discovered Rimbaud, Huxley, and Blake. Each book led to another, and I embarked on the road of self-education.

As I became more confident in my playing, I longed to form a band. I tagged along several times with a friend who rehearsed at a local studio. If picking up the guitar was my first step on the path of a new life, this was the important second step. I met the manager of the studio, Len. He was a talented drummer who played in a Beatles cover band. He was looking to bring someone in to help run the studio and offered me a job, which I happily accepted. It was here I befriended many other local musicians and eventually met the girls with whom I formed my first band.

Len treated me as an equal and had faith I would do a good job. He trusted me and became a mentor. I opened and closed the studio, managed all the bookings, set up the rooms for the bands, kept the place clean, troubleshot sound if needed, and handled the payments. I often arrived early and, after setting everything up, picked one of the rooms to sing or play my guitar in until the first band arrived. I was like a kid again, singing my heart out into my bedroom mirror, but this time I had a real microphone rather than a hairbrush.

Many local bands came in to rehearse there, and I loved being a part of the community. There was a lounge area in the back of the building by the office, where I spent much time in conversation with a diverse group of musicians, artists, and thinkers. It seemed like I belonged there. I ran the studio smoothly, without a hitch, and had great relationships with our clients.

I met Michele, a bass player from Brooklyn, at the studio and we quickly hit it off. Through the studio community, Michele and I met Christine, another guitar player. We soon formed our first band. We played together at the studio, learning songs and writing our own. We hung out all the time and eventually found a drummer. I took over the job of singer; I think it was simply because I could yell the loudest.

My first hint of spirituality started to peek through around this time, with influence from certain books, music, and psychedelics. After that first sugar cube melted, the experience of altered states of consciousness and enhanced sensory perception woke me up to a new world. My deep interest in esoteric matters commenced, and I started writing poetry and lyrics.

The heavy weight of the ideology of Catholicism, which had left a deep aversion to spirituality in any form, lightened. Thinking we humans were more than just skin and bones, a larger picture emerged. I realized there must be a deeper meaning to life, and I questioned and pondered this. My faith as a child was artificial and steeped in fear. It was imposed upon me. I had no connection on a personal level until it was lost completely. I learned faith was what was left after your forced belief system failed and you realized you had no connection to it at all.

I read Buddhist philosophy in my early twenties. It made sense to me, and I naturally flowed toward it. I understood suffering, craving, and the failure to see the world clearly, all of which led me to feelings of despair and dissatisfaction. It made sense to me how if you could see the world clearly—your true self, not your ego self—you could relieve suffering.

Buddhism is a form of self-discovery, which comes from examining one's own experiences and drawing logical conclusions from them. It is about finding your essence, your universal soul that never dies, and liberating yourself from the trappings of life. This does not mean you need to sit and meditate all day; it means you need to learn how to see things distinctly, understand what suffering is, and acknowledge your participation in it. I learned it is up to us as individuals to determine what experience we will have on this earth and in this lifetime. We live in an imperfect world by design. It is the only way to stir our souls to reach the quest to find our authentic selves. Many people never do and will relive suffering repeatedly until lessons are learned.

I was slowly reorganizing my mind, although it would take many more years of growth to make the progress I needed.

It was at the studio where I learned of Music Row in Manhattan at Forty-Eighth Street, between Sixth and Seventh Avenues, the epicenter of music in New York City. I made plans to visit Manny's, the most famous music store on the block, in the entire country, perhaps even the world. While there, I asked on a whim if they had any job openings. This whim was a serendipitous moment; I was hired to work at the accessories counter selling strings, picks, and related items. Manny's was the next decisive step on my journey. There I met Peter, a talented drummer who would, in a defining moment, fill in for our drummer, who backed out days before a scheduled recording session. This moment opened the path to the next dozen years of playing music with Peter, who became like a brother to me.

Forty-Eighth Street was the ultimate place for musicians worldwide, from beginners to professionals. Everyone wanted to visit the famous shops and be part of this definitive music community. It was for all musicians, from the subway and street buskers, Broadway musicians, garage bands, punk bands, rock bands, and metal bands, to the jazz greats, blues masters, and many of the most famous musicians in the world. It was an immersive world of music stores, studios, and repair shops.

I saved to purchase a black ESP Horizon with a Floyd Rose, just like Kirk Hammett of Metallica played. He visited the store often, and I had the opportunity to meet him one day. I had been sitting in the back of the store, playing the opening lick from "Break on Through" by The Doors, when I turned to see him standing there. He was pleasant, delicately shook my hand, and commented on my playing. I thanked him for being an inspiration to me. His guitar playing was the spark that steered me in the direction of my greater path. His words meant so much more than he could have ever imagined. I left work that day with brazen satisfaction.

Working at Manny's was like a dream. Thousands of autographed pictures of every famous musician who had been through the doors hung on the walls. My colleagues became a pack of big-brother friends. I met many of my idols there, most notably Miles Davis. I saw him walk in and go straight to Dilly in the horn department. I watched from across the store as Dilly talked with *Miles Davis*. Dilly caught my eye and motioned for me to come over. I took a breath and walked toward them.

He introduced us: "Miles, this is Kat. Kat, meet Miles Davis."

I did not know what to do; I barely got the word "hello" out of my mouth. His hand was moving to the handshake position.

Inside my head, I was screaming, *I am going to touch Miles Davis's hand*!

I lifted my arm to reach his and he gently held my hand and said, in a barely audible and raspy voice, "Hello, baby."

I smiled, looked right into his eyes, and managed to whisper the word, "Hello," matching his tone, but I was quickly interrupted by someone who recognized him, pushed their way in, and stood in front of me. I walked away and returned to my post, watching while Dilly tried to shield Miles Davis from the interrupter.

Dilly was a horn player, a cat. He called me Kat and was genuine and kind. Spending time with him led me to dive deep into jazz. I was already familiar with John Coltrane, my all-time favorite Billie Holiday, and other well-known jazz musicians, but Dilly led me to explore Thelonious Monk and many more.

As Miles Davis left the store, he turned and nodded at me. He passed away soon after. I spent the next few months incessantly listening to *Kind of Blue*, *Sketches of Spain*, and *Bitches Brew*.

There were many famous musicians who visited Manny's. My foray into the Blues came from Bo Diddley. I had my head down at the counter one day, strumming lightly on a guitar, when I heard someone approaching and looked up and saw the hat.

He smiled and said, "You gotta play the blues, baby."

We had a few laughs. He was friendly and sweet and off I went into the blues—Howlin' Wolf, Muddy Waters, Elmore James, John Lee Hooker, and Robert Johnson, who famously sold his soul to the devil at the crossroads. I could feel the blues in my belly. I knew all about feeling blue.

The hat I instantly recognized now resides in the Smithsonian's National Museum of African American History and Culture.

However, my time at Manny's did not last long. I was becoming exhausted, not sleeping, staying out all night, drinking too much, and still making poor choices about certain people I let into my life. Bad decisions, no boundaries, and my ever-present knack for people-pleasing remained in the way. Still, what I received in return for my brief time there shaped my life and catapulted me to the next and most important part of my journey.

After recording our demo, Christine moved on to go to school and pursue other interests while Michele, Peter, and I formed our band, TreeHouse. It became my life over the next decade, and I devoted all of myself and my time to the band. Peter brought a jazz and progressive rock influence, and, mixed with our quest for a heavy thrash-metal sound, we found our own unique blend. He introduced us to bands like King Crimson and Mahavishnu Orchestra, and we soon were well versed in odd time signatures and multitudes of riffs.

Manny's sold to Sam Ash Music in 1999 and eventually closed in 2009. The rest of the shops on the block followed suit, and the once-vibrant area is now a characterless landscape filled with expensive apartments and hotels. The landscape of New York City has changed drastically since the fall of Forty-Eighth Street.

Rezoning and huge development projects took over, and many cultural landmarks and historic buildings were lost. These places had made the city what it was. The dive bars and odd mom-and-pop shops, which were the souls of neighborhoods, were replaced with chain stores and soulless gleaming skyscrapers with high-priced apartments only the wealthy could afford. These were not the natural changes of an evolving city benefiting all its residents but the results of actions taken to ensure maximum profits through insatiable greed.

The character, charm, and atmosphere of many sections of the city have been radically changed. I am so grateful I was able to experience the city as it was before the displacement of its culture to please newcomers and tourists by erasing socioeconomic diversity.

It quickly became clear I would not be able to maintain my life in the band without a better-paying job. A friend who worked as a legal secretary suggested I give it a try. In the administrative world, working at a law firm was a chance to make a good salary. I found a six-month business school that offered a legal-administrative course. I worked during the day, went to school three nights per week, and went to band practice the remaining nights. After completing the course, I found a job at a small law firm on Staten Island. I wanted to gain experience before moving to a larger firm in Manhattan.

My simple goal was to familiarize myself with the field, make enough money to live, and cover my share of our studios' monthly rent. In hindsight, this was the next important step on my journey and the second time I was mentored by someone I grew to greatly admire, an attorney named Bill. He was in his early sixties, a recovered alcoholic, and an extremely thoughtful person who held an immense sense of humor, compassion, and intellect. We bonded quickly, and I did well at my job.

We spent hours discussing a variety of topics. He saw in me what no one else had. In the relatively short time we spent together, I learned more from him than I had in the first two decades of my life. My self-education accelerated greatly. My interest in literature and reading fast-tracked during my time with Bill. He encouraged me to read, since reading was the key to learning. He recommended the classics, such as *Moby-Dick*, *Catcher in the Rye*, and *The Scarlet Letter*. We discussed characters and plot and imagined other, more farcical endings.

The office had a large window with a view of the Verrazano Bridge, the Hudson River, and Brooklyn. Many of our conversations took place at his desk, next to the window, and he often diverted the conversation to point out the beauty of the clouds, the color of the sky, or the way the sun shone off the water.

Before becoming a lawyer, Bill had been a chemist working for Mobil Oil; he often tied nature's bountiful beauty to chemistry lessons. He asked random questions like, "Do you know why the sky is blue?"

We discussed the earth's atmosphere, gases, particles, and how blue light scatters and travels in smaller waves. After these conversations, I read related magazines or went to the library to learn more, so that the next time it came up, I had something to add to the conversation.

Bill's appreciation of nature, art, and music helped me not only to fully see it but to understand the details too. He sparked my initiative to learn. I saw him for what he truly was, not through his past and other people's verdicts, and he saw me for the same. Not long after I started, he sent me to do research at the courthouse and report my findings back to him. I quickly became familiar with his practice and was drafting documents and successfully performing a higher level of work in a short period of time. He saw potential in me and encouraged me to go to law school, but I was deeply embedded in the band and my life in music and could not imagine having the time to go back to school or the money to pay for it.

The *New York Times* arrived each morning at the office, and I often browsed through it before he arrived. If it had not been opened and read by the time he came in, he put it back on my desk, saying "Read the *Times* every day, kid. It's important."

Besides heaps of coffee, the paper's daily crossword puzzle was the official start of the day. He called me in if he was stuck on a clue. I doubt he was ever baffled; it was just another opportunity for him to teach. I still read the *Times* every day and get through as much of the crossword puzzle as possible.

We listened to classical music all day while in the office. The only other time I had been exposed to classical music was in the soft velvety seats in the back of my aunt and uncles' fancy car, where the radio was always tuned in to the classical station. I had no further spark of interest of my own in the genre. But we sat and listened intently to certain pieces, discussed the emotional aspects of the compositions, and compared each composer's style and nuances. I grew to love classical music. On Friday mornings, we listened to Mozart's Requiem—surely one of the most beautiful compositions ever written, and whose remarkable story I became and remain completely obsessed with.[4]

We examined the great artists the same way we examined the great composers. He encouraged me to visit the Met, the MoMA, and the Guggenheim, which I did and grew to love.

One day, I was sitting at my desk and a large package arrived. Bill walked out of his office and excitedly opened the box while explaining what was inside. It was Salvador Dalí's *Lincoln in Dalivision*, the famous lithograph based on Dalí's painting *Gala Contemplating the Mediterranean Sea*, which when viewed from a distance of twenty meters is transformed into a portrait of Abraham Lincoln. Bill hung it up on the wall at the end of the long hallway, which he had measured beforehand to ensure the required floor length. Twenty meters or twenty-six steps. The painting depicts the back of a nude female standing and looking out toward the sun setting over the sea. As the viewer steps back from the painting, the blocks surrounding her become recognizable as the face of Abraham Lincoln. As you get farther away, the woman disappears, and only the impression of Lincoln remains.

As we stood at the end of the hallway looking at the face of Lincoln, Bill explained how Dalí and the genre of surrealism were an exploration of the subconscious.

The mind can perceive things that aren't there. Sometimes a painful past, fear, and other negative thoughts can become influential in holding you back from realizing your true potential.

Every Friday, Bill went to the track, and just about every day he visited the local Off-Track Betting (OTB). Horse racing was another area of interest, and I learned the many stats to take into consideration when selecting a horse, from the horse's record to the weight of the jockey. Even with his expert guidance, I secretly just picked the horses whose names I liked. When he could not make it to OTB, I went for him. He was convinced I was his lucky charm because every time I went, we won. All the other OTB regulars came to know me and my lucky streak and would approach me after leaving the betting window to see which horses I picked.

The first time I accompanied Bill to the track was when he had cataract surgery on one of his eyes and could not drive. The day after the surgery was a Friday, and he came into the office with a patch over his right eye, dropped his car keys on my desk, and said, "Let's go, kid, we are going to the track."

My first thought was that I had never driven on the dreaded Brooklyn-Queens Expressway, the always-crowded and under-perpetual-construction road we had to take to get to the track. I was a city kid; I took the bus or the subway everywhere. I had only ever driven locally, with the "company" car Bill let me use.

When I expressed my fear, he said, "You're going to have to do it someday. No time like the present, so let's go."

We headed to Aqueduct Racetrack on the border of Queens and Long Island. The drive was fine and one we made many times after that. Our lucky streak continued; my first trip to the track paid off with a couple of hundred-dollar wins. Sometimes we sat inside, ordered snacks and drinks, and watched from the windows or the close-up on the giant screens. Other times we stood at the fence a few feet from the track and yelled to the jockeys when they came into the paddock at the end of the race. We had great conversations during the drive back and forth.

He became the father figure I never had, and during our relationship I learned more from him than I had from anyone. I appreciated him.

After a year or so, things soured at the office with Bill's partners, and I was let go. In the end, perhaps our chummy relationship did not sit so well with others, or maybe they just knew I was completely stoned all the time. During our parting conversation, Bill reiterated how he wanted me to go back to school. He affirmed that no matter what, I was moving on to "bigger and better things." No one had ever spoken to me in a way that made me see the potential I had. Thanks to him, I was absolutely prepared.

We kept in touch over the years. Our last conversation was in 2008, when I told him how much his mentoring meant to me and the difference it made in my life. He passed away a few years later.

Since I had experience working as a legal secretary under my belt, I took the leap into the larger law firm world in Manhattan. I spent most of my time in our studio in Hell's Kitchen, and it was more convenient to work in the city. Through a recruiter, I went on a few interviews and was hired by a firm named Thacher, Proffitt & Wood. The offices were in the South Tower of the World Trade Center and occupied floors thirty-eight through forty. The day I interviewed was my first time in the buildings I had seen from every vantage point throughout my life. They were the giant two front teeth of the city visible from many miles away. While waiting in the reception area, I read a book on the sofa table about the history of the firm. Founded in 1848 and originally located on Wall Street, the firm represented surviving passengers from the *Titanic*. Fascinating.

I was initially hired as a floater, covering for other secretaries, but quickly secured a permanent spot in the Structured Finance Group on the fortieth floor. I excelled at my job and found myself in a new world, enjoying spending time with my colleagues in and out of the office, all of whom were smart, interesting, and kind people. The group dominated the securitization and structured finance market by advising clients in the packaging and selling of mortgage-backed securities. I quickly found my footing in the work and made friends. My mask came in handy, and I blended in as best I could. It seemed everyone came from a good family, had a good education, and was blessed with comfortable lives. I pretended I did too.

I loved working in the WTC. The view from our office was amazing. Many times, I stood and stared out the window, looking out at the entire city spread out before me, wondering how

I'd managed to get there. Looking south toward the Statue of Liberty, the sunsets were the most beautiful I had ever seen.

My desk in the WTC was where I took the next leaps in my self-education. During downtime, I read the books a colleague, who held an unmatched love of books and reading, recommended. After some time, I gave him some of my lyrics to read, which he complimented and compared to Rimbaud. I had read a bit of Rimbaud after learning of his work through a Jim Morrison biography several years prior. *A Season in Hell* became a favorite. My desk soon had a corner filled with books by authors I had never heard of before.

At night, I spent my time with musicians and artists, and during the day I spent my time with lawyers. Many other staff members of the firm were artists, musicians, writers, or actors who'd also found their way to work as legal secretaries because the pay was good enough to support their low- or nonpaying passions.

At TPW, I found myself in a setting where I was able to take my self-education to the next level. What I loved about our group was how they were just as comfortable in a Michelin-rated restaurant as they were in a dive bar. I realized how a secure upbringing provided a feeling of comfort and a sense of fitting in anywhere. "Normal" people seemed so relaxed.

I worked overtime when it was available to make extra money. Being in the WTC at night was quite different than the daytime, when the buildings were at full capacity and the outside hustled and bustled. The city that never sleeps does quiet a bit at night, allowing its beauty to shine through uninterrupted. Without the sounds of a full office to damper and distract, the creaking of the building was more audible and the movement from the wind more noticeable. The towers, due to their height, were designed to sway to absorb wind, which caused the steel columns to creak lightly. In heavy winds, the top of the building could sway up to twelve inches. We sometimes felt a slight movement on our floor, but most of the time it almost seemed imagined. It was just too scary to think the entire building was moving!

From my place at the window, the city lights sparkled in the darkness, reaching in all directions for miles, and cast a seemingly supernatural glow, making it appear otherworldly. Without the many distractions of daylight, perception changed, and the darkness narrowed focus. My vantage point high above the city streets made me feel like anything was possible for me now. I lived in the greatest city in the world.

Chapter Five

RESURGET EX FAVILLA

Throughout 1991, the transformation of Times Square from the gritty, crime-ridden area of porno theaters, peep shows, and open-air drug sales slowly gave way to a family-friendly tourist destination with hotels, theme stores, and restaurants. Three blocks south of Forty-Second Street, TreeHouse rented rehearsal space in the Music Building, a twelve-story structure on Eighth Avenue, which bordered Hell's Kitchen and the Garment District. The Music Building was created in 1979; it provided 24/7 access to rehearsal space through sublets or monthly rentals. It was one of a kind and a fixture of the local music scene. Every musician in the city came through its doors. Over the years, some had successful careers. It also hosted thousands of bands the world would never know, the many talented songwriters and artists who formed a community in the building.

As musicians, we tightened up our playing by working continuously in the studio. When friends hung out downtown, we rehearsed in the studio. As TreeHouse grew as a band, the neighborhood around us grew as well. The area was still not the safest place to be walking around late at night, but it surely kept me on my toes. Michele and I usually walked to the subway together. On occasion, when alone, I jogged all the way there. Thanks to my hypervigilant inner danger sensor, I knew intuitively which block to turn on, what side of the street to walk on, and which subway car to enter or switch to mid-ride. I had a knack for sensing threats. At first, I did not always listen, but each time I did not, I found myself in a precarious situation. I learned to listen and remove myself from potential hazards. Perhaps every New Yorker developed these skills over time.

Traveling alone late at night after rehearsal or gigs had its downside, and I did find myself in compromising positions on occasion. I was steeped in street smarts so could manage my way around them. I wore headphones, so if anyone said anything to me, I could pretend I did not hear. However, I always carried a guitar strapped to my back and a book in my hand and often had great conversations with random interesting people during my travels.

Playing in this band saved my life. The rage, which fueled my thunderous singing, sounded like what had happened to me. It was the embodiment of the intolerable pain I carried in my body and of which only I was privy to. Playing and singing such ferocious music helped to release the demons who secretly resided in me, the unbearable memories, and the unrelenting pain I stored within my body. I wore T-shirts and jeans most of the time, the opposite of the uniform of the typical girl band, clad in the Lower East Side uniform of leather, cleavage, bondage gear, and heavy makeup. I did not hold that type of fashion bravery or show-womanship. Michele and I were adamant that our music rather than our looks be the focus, a notion we held right from the start. We wanted to be great musicians, and we rehearsed five nights a week to reach our goal.

Once we had a solid set of songs, we started gigging. Our first show was set up by a friend. It was in Queens at an outdoor event. When we arrived, we saw it was a biker party and became nervous. It took guts to get up in front of the crowd, but we performed our set. It was a great introduction to playing live . . . not because they loved us—they did not know what to think— but they were kind enough and impressed with our surprising ferocity. A few from the audience became friends and showed up at many gigs over the years. I remember thinking that if I could get through that, I could get through anything.

Standing onstage at famous venues like CBGB, performing at lesser-known holes-in-the-wall, or rehearsing in our studio gave me the same sense of satisfaction and fulfillment. Although terribly shy, over the years I became more comfortable. When I played my guitar and sang, I was durable and compelling, but in between songs I shrank into myself. Those few seconds between songs seemed like forever. I did not necessarily like being onstage and the focus of attention, but the result was an intrinsic and therapeutic indulgence I had never experienced before.

I spent over a decade screaming as the singer and guitar player of TreeHouse. It was an unplanned, highly effective way to release the trauma I held. As I look back at the lyrics and poetry I was writing, I realize my entire body of work was filled with hints about my past. After one night out with friends, I woke up on the couch in our studio to a pounding headache and gray skies and wrote:

In the gray morning I woke
Startled
I spoke broken words
And lost hope in the world
Choked on misguided thoughts
A thousand and one of sorts
Please understand
It's not what it seems
My world is a world of lies
They are hidden behind my eyes

You only know the me
that I pretend to see
You'll never know my grief
Not in your wildest dreams
A thief stole my leaf of peace
Now I am the seller of secrets
I lost my precious gold
I could not hold
Onto me

As time went on, the band took me from victim to warrior, albeit a warrior with hidden secrets. I learned about primal scream therapy from a story about John Lennon's experience with it.

Primal Scream is a trauma-based psychotherapy created by Arthur Janov, which became influential in the early 1970s after the publication of his first book, *The Primal Scream*. It claims that expressing normally repressed anger and frustration through unrestrained screams is a way to extract emotional pain and its long-lasting psychological effects.

I was highly skilled at turning my vocals into a beneficial and curative primal scream.

Peter, Michele, and I, and what became our tight circle of friends, grew close over the years. Our small group of confidants and supporters became like family and were our staunch advocates. They helped us move our gear in and out of the studio and set up venues for gigs. We spent a lot of time together celebrating birthdays and holidays. I had a supportive circle of allies I could trust and depend on. We formed our larger TreeHouse community with many other close friends, bands who shared our studio space, other musicians in the building, and friends from Forty-Eighth Street, and we each wholeheartedly supported one another's projects.

The TreeHouse studio in the Music Building was also known for its epic parties, on special occasions or no occasion at all. There were many raucous revelries until a friend was stuck on the roof on New Year's Eve. After going up to get some fresh air, the door slammed shut and locked behind him. No one heard him banging on the door or yelling from the rooftop. It was a freezing-cold night, and he was not wearing a coat. He made it into the top elevator-shaft room by breaking a window, which helped him to survive the night. He was discovered the next morning by the security person. We bore the responsibility for his ordeal and were grateful it did not end badly. The parties simmered down afterward.

One day, I stepped into the elevator and pressed ten. I heard footsteps and stopped the doors from closing so the person could get on. It was Sean Lennon. We greeted each other and smiled. I was amazed by how much he looked like his father. Before I could think of anything to say, the elevator stopped, and he said to me, "Goodbye. Have a pleasant evening."

I said, "Thanks, same to you." It was a thrilling moment. It was normal for famous musicians to be in the building. Madonna, who had been a resident in the early 1980s, once came in while filming a documentary and signed her name on the wall of the floor she spent time on. They preserved it by covering it with a square of thick plastic.

Peter was friends with many well-known drummers he'd met while working at Manny's for many years. They'd often stop into our studio to visit. He knew many of the greats, including one of whom who at the time was playing with Lou Reed. They'd be rehearsing at the building for an upcoming gig. One afternoon, I took the stairs to their floor and stood in the hallway outside of their room. I heard the unmistakable voice of Lou Reed! Those moments inspired and exhilarated me.

Another visitor to our studio was a drummer who played for one of the late-night shows on television. He was an amazing musician, and his joy was contagious. After hearing us for the first time, he said to Peter, "Those ladies ain't no joke!" One of the nicest compliments we ever received.

Through a friend's connection, an opportunity arose to buy some of the equipment backline of the band Manowar. They were selling old gear they held in their warehouse in Upstate New York. Manowar was known for many things: being a 1980s metal band, soaring anthems based on sword-and-sorcery fantasy, and even a guest narrator appearance by the legendary Orson Welles on their song "Dark Avenger." But what drew us into wanting their equipment was their 1984 entrance into the *Guinness Book of World Records* for the loudest performance, a record they broke on two further occasions. A friend and I drove upstate in a borrowed van and picked up eight speaker cabinets. We now had in our arsenal a portion of the backline of the loudest band in the world. Check.

We spent all our free time at the Music Building in our studio. All the while, I was covertly making progress in purging myself of the traumas of what had happened to me. People made comments on how normal I seemed, yet I was able to create this earsplitting and rumbling scream, which was anything but.

There was often police activity outside the Music Building, so much that after a while on our nightly walks to the corner deli, we hardly noticed. One summer night, Michele and I opened the front door, and we stepped out into the flashing lights of several police cars. A woman was running around completely naked in the street. Traffic was stopped, and several police officers were trying to catch her. Everyone on the sidewalk stopped to watch the action. Although this was a step up from the usual crazy, we still just kept walking and watching as we went by. As we exited the store, she ran by us and slid under a parked box truck. Several officers surrounded it.

We watched and walked, and I heard, "Kath"!

One of the officers was a friend from grammar school I had not seen in ages. Though the scene was chaotic and depressing, it was nice to see an old friend at the same time.

We chatted for a moment before the other officers yelled, "She's throwing shit! She's throwing it!"

He calmly said, "Great to see you, but I guess I'd better get back to work."

Michele and I left, strolling back to the building and continuing our conversation while chaos ensued. Often during these walks, I thought about telling her the truth about what had happened to me as a child, how TreeHouse and our friendship had saved my life. I had come close a few times but always backed off at the last moment. It was too heavy, and I just wasn't ready. Instead, I used clues in our song lyrics: "The seller of secrets is the teller of lies . . . She hides them there behind her eyes . . . So you can't see." The clues only I knew were clues.

We gigged steadily. The crowds who came to see us grew larger. We wanted our show to be entertaining and invited friends or special guests to join us for a song. Peter came across a musician who played the bagpipe in one of the tunnels under Grand Central Station. He joined us for a Saint Patrick's Day gig. The bagpipes were earsplitting in the small club.

We did a Halloween show where a friend dressed as Michael Myers from the movie *Halloween*. He hid behind the amps onstage as we played the movie's theme song. When we reached a certain part, we piped in Jamie Lee Curtis's scream, which was the cue for him to step out and pretend to slit Michele's throat with a plastic knife filled with fake blood. As we started the first song of the set, he grabbed a pumpkin filled with candy and threw it out to the crowd.

The brightest moment was when a girl approached me and Michele and said, "I just got a guitar because of you."

Other times, some jerk who was unfamiliar with us yelled, "Show us your tits!" It only served to make me more ferocious, and once we started playing, the offender quickly left. We weren't there to turn people on; we were there to rip their faces off.

The Lower East Side scene during the 1990s was filled with poets, punks, bands, artists, squatter tenements, and a diverse community pulsating with life. The grittiness was still there, not like it was in the 1970s and 1980s, but the area held its characteristics. This was the last decade before complete gentrification.

Being in a band was a dream come true. In the beginning, I was determined to get us signed by a label, make records, and tour, but after a while, it became less important. Just making music, writing songs and lyrics, and playing gigs made me feel happy and content. I was satisfied with how I found this path that pulled me out of a hole so deep, it was absolutely a miracle I was not completely swallowed by it. We had moments when there could have been a chance for a record deal or representation, but it did not pan out. In hindsight, it was not designed to go any further. And I did realize the greatest achievement from playing in this band was how it transformed and restored me. It cleansed me of the bulk of negative emotions I held in my heart. It formed an opening in my psyche and inserted the healing medicine of music and community. It was not about success or failure; it was a spiritual practice.

We stayed together for over a decade, through lots of ups and downs. Toward the end, things were getting harder and more frustrating. A band is like a marriage, and they end for similar reasons when things get too hard for too long. We held on for as long as we could, but when it was over, it was over, and the end was grueling. All was lost, including my treasured friendship with Michele.

I had a complete yet quiet breakdown when TreeHouse ended. I did not know what to do with my life without it. But, every ending is a new beginning, and I soon stepped further into my future, serendipitously, once again. I randomly walked around the city like I had as a kid and one day ended up on Sixth Street between First and Second Avenues. This section of Sixth Street was filled with Indian restaurants. The aromas in the air were amazing, but what caught my attention was the music. In each restaurant's front window sat a sitar player, most, but not all, accompanied by a tabla player. I was familiar with the sitar and Indian classical music through The Beatles, namely George Harrison, but something sparked inside of me that day. I returned repeatedly to Sixth Street to listen. I was fascinated and drawn to the sitar. I ordered a student model online. I ordered books on Indian classical music and a basic how-to book by Ravi Shankar, who I listened to incessantly.

One afternoon, I went to Forty-Eighth Street to one of the shops to see if they carried tablas, the small hand drums used to accompany sitar. It was there I met Alex, my future husband and life partner. We had an instant connection; I had never been surer of anything in my life.

As our relationship progressed, I came to realize how love—true love—sometimes includes taking risks and the willingness to change a false self. If mutual, love has the power to make important and progressive changes through the learning of life lessons. Love expands, it does not contract, it reshapes, and it is the path to growth. I did not grow up dreaming of getting married or having children, white picket fences, or happily ever after. I did not believe I was eligible for them. In the world I grew up in, they did not exist. But something was different this time, and I could not walk away, even though I tried.

When TreeHouse ended, Peter and I carried on without Michele and found a new bass player. She was talented, and although musically I was excited with what we produced, it never seemed right. I knew that my desire to continue after the ending of TreeHouse was purely based on my fear of losing the only part of my life where I found real purpose. I continued for a few more years, even though I knew in my heart it was over.

Soon after my thirtieth birthday, I met Ravi Shankar. A small audience was allowed to attend a performance at CBS Studios in Midtown, where Ravi and his daughter, Anoushka, were recording a segment for the CBS morning show. I arrived early to the studio on Fifty-Seventh Street and was the first person admitted inside. There were just a few rows of chairs set up in front of a small stage. I sat in the first chair in the front row. The studio buzzed as the production got underway, with stagehands setting up microphones and producers giving directions. I had met many famous musicians over the last decade, but this was different.

Ravi and Anoushka stepped onto the small stage. After bowing toward the audience, they sat and began to play. The performance was exhilarating from my seat just a few feet away. I was deeply inspired by every note. Afterward, I was able to say hello to Ravi. He was kind and generous with his time. When we shook hands, I thought of his relationship with George Harrison and all the points where the Beatles connected to my life. We took a photograph together. It remains one of my most prized possessions. I explained I had recently started to learn the sitar and mentioned how much I loved it. It was a moment of life-changing inspiration.

I found a teacher in the city right away. Indian classical music became and remains to this day a true medicine for my soul. It helped me stabilize. I was enraptured by its complex history, traditions, and rituals. As a guitar player and singer in a metal band for many years, where I battered my guitar and screamed my rage up and out of my body, my bones were released from the grips of trauma. As a student of Indian classical music, playing sitar gently settled my bones back into their rightful place.

The loss of my friendship with Michele, who was like a sister to me, and my decision to move on to a new band left me with feelings of regret. It had been almost one year since our last tense conversation, and I decided to reach out to her to see if we could talk. I had hoped our friendship retained strong roots that could hold it up until it could be repaired. We didn't know it yet, but on the horizon was an unthinkable moment of surreal sadness and utter disaster that changed all our lives forever and made it clear which direction I needed to walk toward.

Chapter Six

A SCREAMING COMES ACROSS THE SKY

Tuesday, September 11, 2001, was a mild September morning with a cloudless and vibrant blue sky. It was the kind of weather that made you want to take the day off from work and head to a park to soak up the last bits of warmth before the cooler air of fall settled in. As I left my apartment to go to work, I planned to at least sit in the courtyard for lunch. I was commuting alone that morning; Alex had some errands to run and was driving to Queens.

I left the apartment to catch the 8:30 a.m. ferry. I boarded the boat, sat in a quiet area, and settled in comfortably so I could start a new book, *Gravity's Rainbow* by Thomas Pynchon. I was surely torturing myself with its famously complicated plotlines and characters. I held it in my hands, feeling the weight of its pages, and stared at the missile on the cover. I opened the book and read the first line: "A screaming comes across the sky."

The approach of the Statue of Liberty was my cue to start gathering my belongings, as there were only a few minutes left in the ride, but on this morning, as Lady Liberty came into view, a panicked shouting came across the ferry with several people loudly yelling, "The World Trade Center is on fire!"

Everyone immediately looked up; some ran to the windows. My gaze connected with a woman who sat across from me.

She caught my eyes and said nervously, "My son is a firefighter in Brooklyn. I'm sure he's on his way over there."

I stood and quickly walked to the back of the boat, stepped outside, and leaned over the edge. As I looked toward the city, I saw with absolute disbelief a massive ball of flame and thick black smoke shooting out of the top portion of Tower One. A flurry of speculation and nervousness erupted all around. What happened? It must have been a plane crash, a terrible accident. The sky was so blue and clear; visibility was perfect. How could a plane crash into the building?

As the ferry neared the slip, I stared at Tower One on fire. I hoped my colleagues who arrived early to the office in Tower Two evacuated quickly. It was a few minutes before 9:00 a.m. when the ferry pulled into the dock, right on schedule, but the departing wary passengers were unusually quiet and slow. No one pushed by to beat the crowd to the subway. A strange heaviness of unspecified fear and speculation as to what was happening hung in the air.

I walked past the subway entrance toward the side of Battery Park, watching the flames shoot from the building and the smoke fill the sky. I continued toward the towers, assuming I would meet up with colleagues within the outer perimeter of the complex or at our designated emergency meeting place a few blocks away along the Hudson River. My cell phone rang. It was one of my closest friends, Cissy, who was home and watching the news.

"A plane hit Tower One. Do not go to your office. Something is going on here," she said.

We spoke for a minute, sharing our disbelief at what was happening, and just as I hung up, a booming noise roared out of nowhere. A giant jet thundering across the sky appeared just above the treetops of Battery Park. The trees shook and the ground trembled. I had to steady my body as the force of the jet engines' thrust enveloped everything below it. Startled, I could clearly see the logo, United Airlines, in blue lettering. The aircraft was so near to the ground that the windows were visible. I screamed, "Where is that plane going? Why is it flying so low? What is happening!" From my vantage point, the buildings across the street from the park blocked out a portion of the view of Tower Two. I could still see the flames and dark black smoke rising out of Tower One, and as I lost sight of the jet, in the next split second, another huge explosion and fireball poured into the sky. This was not an accident.

People on the street around me screamed and ran in all directions, back toward the ferry, into the park, anywhere away from what we had just witnessed. I stood in complete shock for a moment until a woman standing next to me grabbed my hand, and we ran back toward the ferry together. It was complete chaos among the hundreds of passengers who just minutes ago had made their way off the ferry and were now rushing to get back on. *What just happened?* was rushing through my mind as I ran. It was terrifying. The deckhands were standing at the entrance, yelling for everyone to get on the boat. We ran on together, the anonymous woman and I, still holding hands. We hugged and separated, wishing for each other to be safe. I stood on the deck and watched as crowds of people ran onto the boat. Alex was driving on the BQE and did not have a cell phone. I had no way to let him know I was not in the building. I wondered if he knew what was happening.

The ferry waited for as many people to board as possible before departing. What was next? The Statue of Liberty, the Empire State Building, the Stock Exchange, the ferryboat I was standing on? This huge bright-orange boat could be seen from space. It crossed my mind that I should stay outside. If the boat was hit, I could jump off and swim. It was approximately 9:20 a.m. when the boat engines started to accelerate. As we pulled out of the slip, the full view of a mutilated downtown Manhattan slowly came into view. I will never forget the sheer terror of that scene. Paper and debris floated in the air like during the ticker-tape parades down Broadway when the Yankees won a World Series. The flames and black smoke poured out of the floors of the towers that were impacted. I overheard transmissions crackling from the boat crew's walkie-talkies.

"Terrorist attack. All New York City tunnels and bridges shut down. All subways and buses shut down. Advise passengers to put on life jackets. Repeat. Advise passengers to put on life jackets."

I stared at Tower Two, trying to count the floors where the plane hit. I envisioned huge bursts of explosions and fire in our office. In my mind, I saw my desk, the surrounding walls, offices, and the photos of smiling colleagues and their loved ones on each desk burning. As I tried to calculate how long it might take to walk down forty flights of stairs, depending on how crowded the staircase was, an announcement came over the loudspeakers: "All passengers are advised to put on life jackets." It repeated twice, slower the second time. Some people moved quickly to heed the call, but others, including myself, were frozen in a moment of shock and disbelief. As we neared the Statue of Liberty, I stared at it, like I had a thousand times before, but this time was different. Was it the next target?

My phone rang. It was Mother, who had moved to another state to live with my sibling a year prior. They were watching the news. She was frantic, hysterical; she thought I was dead. After a brief contact, the cell service was quickly overwhelmed by heavy usage and the call dropped. More commotion arose as people frantically tried to make sense of what we'd all just witnessed.

Someone shouted, "Another one! Another attack! A plane just hit the Pentagon!"

People cried out for loved ones who worked in the towers. A deckhand passed out life jackets to passengers who did not have them. I took one from his shaking hands, held it to my chest, and braced for impact.

The ferry ride across the Hudson River to Staten Island on this surreal morning was like a slow-moving funeral procession. As the ferry pulled into the slip, passengers quickly departed, stepping off into a chilling and unfamiliar new world. A man in a business suit was walking along the slip with a cell phone at his ear, crying, screaming, "My wife is dead! My wife is dead!" It was the first time I cried that morning.

Fearing the ferry terminal could be a target, I avoided entering the building and walked outside, up the car ramp, and one block to our apartment. I sat dumbfounded and in shock at what I saw on the television screen. Both towers burning. Images of people watching from the streets below in absolute horror at the scene unfolding before their eyes. News-helicopter-camera shots of the people who were trapped on floors above or directly below the fires waving pieces of clothing to bring attention to their location. I watched in real time the inconceivable and dreadful choice made by several who were trapped above the flames to jump from the towers. It generated a pure and absolute feeling of horror.

The television screen showed the Pentagon burning, a gaping hole in the structure. Chaos. My phone rang; it was Michele. We had not talked for close to a year. When I heard her voice, I was taken back to the time we saw the Red Hot Chili Peppers at the top of Tower One. I was able to get two tickets through our firm's office manager. The band played to a small crowd of industry people and radio-contest winners to promote a new record. We spoke briefly and planned to meet a few weeks later.

My phone continued to ring throughout the day, concerned calls from friends and family checking to see if I made it out of the building, the relief clearly heard in their voices when I picked up.

I stared at the towers burning on the television screen. It was all sinking in. I noticed one of them was moving strangely, swaying like it usually did in a strong windstorm. Perhaps it was just the camera shot from the news helicopter. With horror, I watched as the tower proceeded to pancake into itself. I realized it was our tower. Tower Two.

The news anchor reported with a voice full of disbelief and dread, "The South Tower is collapsing!"

In rapid succession, one floor at a time, it crumbled. In a matter of seconds, it was gone. The news footage showed a massive cloud of dust and debris consuming the entire area, rushing through the streets like a volcanic eruption covering everything and everyone who could not outrun its swift pace in a fine, gray powder. Our office was gone. I thought again of my colleagues and friends. Were they trapped in the staircase trying to get out? No one still in the building could have survived. My heart sank.

Images of the office played in my mind, first as I remembered them, and second as slow-motion images of everything being slowly pulverized by falling concrete and flames. The large collection of curated artworks and sculptures in our reception area were all gone in a flash. I pictured my desk trinkets and photos; my cherished books full of page-holder sticky notes and pieces of copy paper with lyrics scribbled in a rush stuck inside; the flowers I had picked up the day before, next to my worn and now appropriately titled copy of Rimbaud's *A Season in Hell*—it was now all on fire.

I thought of my fellow tower workers, thousands of them, who I saw each day coming in and out of the building. Familiar faces I shared an elevator ride with or sat next to on a bench in the courtyard. The security guards at the turnstiles, the housekeeping staff, and everyone who was part of the massive complex. The underground mall with stores full of workers and visitors. The day care center, whose caregivers pulled their tiny charges around the complex in a small blue train, bringing smiles to all who passed.

The phone rang again; this time it was a person from another of the firm's offices. They used the firm's phone list to contact each employee and confirm their safety. So far, all had been accounted for. Meanwhile, companies that had offices in the towers were also trying to reach their employees through the local news stations. The scroll at the bottom of the screen showed the company name and a phone number to call to be accounted for.

As I watched the coverage happen in real time, the news anchor flatly stated, "We have another hijacked plane. It crashed into a field in Pennsylvania; it is believed to have been headed to Washington, DC."

The horror of the morning continued with the collapse of the North Tower—another massive cloud of dust and debris. Again, people ran for their lives.

Alex finally walked into the apartment hours later, after being stuck on the BQE, crawling toward the shut-down Verrazano Bridge, where security and police were checking cars before allowing them across. He had a front-row seat to the attack as it unfolded across the Hudson River. He explained that he'd been on his way home when traffic stopped moving after the first plane hit, with drivers pulling over on the shoulder and stepping out of their cars. He saw that one of the towers was on fire but could not tell which one. He feared the worst. While stopped on the side of the expressway, he watched with horror as the second plane hit. He thought I was gone. Getting back in the car in disbelief, he sat in traffic inching toward home as he watched Tower Two fall, soon followed by Tower One. The giant cloud of debris enveloped lower Manhattan and crossed the Hudson River toward the road-way. Pieces of paper filled the sky and flew overhead, landing on the car and the road. The scene was apocalyptic, and by then he was convinced I was dead.

The news reported that Lower Manhattan was being evacuated. All public transportation was shut down. The television showed images of thousands of people walking in the streets and over bridges, trying to make their way home. Many looked like ghosts, covered from head to toe in the dust and ash from the massive plume clouds.

An immediate and spontaneous launch of the largest maritime rescue was also underway. The evacuation of up to half a million people plucked from the waterfront at the edges of Lower Manhattan by the Staten Island Ferry, the water taxis out of New Jersey, the coast guard, the Sandy Hook Pilots, the NYPD tugboats, and any boat that happened to be on the water joined in.

Our apartment was about six miles away from the towers, or what was left of them. The smell of smoke soon became stronger. We shut all the windows and remained glued to the television and telephone the entire day.

Just before dark, we left the apartment to walk to the water's edge. As we exited our building and turned the corner toward the water, seeing the view of Lower Manhattan without the towers there as the focal point was startling. Even though we had been watching the news all day and watched the towers fall, I still could not believe my eyes. They were gone. All that was left in the space was smoke and ash. We stood on the sidewalk above the parking area at the ferry terminal. It was full. Usually, at that time of the evening, commuters returned from their offices and drove away, but that day was different. The cars of people who went to work that morning, many who were never coming home, remained. The fence was gradually being filled with flowers and candles. Alex and I stood in silence, gripping each other's hands, as someone in the crowd played a newscast on a portable radio. As we listened, it was the first time we heard the words "Ground Zero."

As we stared at the fractured skyline, I thought of how the horror of what occurred came out of the clear blue sky. But I also remembered how the emerging reality of violent jihad had infiltrated our shores almost a decade prior.

On February 26, 1993, a box truck entered the basement parking garage under the North Tower of the World Trade Center complex. A bomb inside the truck was detonated, killing six people and injuring over one thousand. The mastermind behind the attack escaped and initiated the planning of far-more-deadly strikes.

The New York City landmark bomb plot, designed to follow the 1993 bombing of the World Trade Center, was disrupted by an FBI informant who infiltrated the group. There were six targets: tunnels and bridges connecting Manhattan to New Jersey; the United Nations; two hotels that catered to visiting diplomats; and the FBI building in Lower Manhattan. The plan took years to develop and if not disrupted could have killed tens of thousands of innocent people. The investigation was lengthy and resulted in the arrest of eight extremists, who were detained while in the process of mixing the chemicals for the bombs.

This was a time of additional security in the subways and at bridge crossings, a sight I became so familiar with after September 11. The case took a long time to prosecute. The story stayed in the news for several years following the arrests.

That night, a dream took me back to the window in our office. Looking out at a perfectly clear and brilliant blue sky over the city, hands pressed against the glass, I noticed a small dot in the distance becoming larger and larger. I heard a sound getting louder and louder as the dot turned into a giant airplane in the space between my hands.

The next day, it was confirmed that every employee of the firm survived. Those who were in the building ignored the announcement by the Port Authority claiming our tower was safe and for persons evacuating to return to their floors. Many of those who listened to those instructions did return and did not make it out. Our firm was one of the few companies in the towers that had not experienced a loss of employees.

A law firm in midtown offered to house our team of attorneys, paralegals, and administrative staff. We met there just three days later. Although it was with heavy hearts, we gathered, thankful to be together. Our belongings, papers, desks, and office were gone, but those are replaceable things. Our hearts and minds were with the thousands of murdered innocents and their loved ones.

Finishing our month's work gave our group a purpose and a sense of control over the most surreal of times. We held on to a perception of continuity as we recreated our documents from scratch, closing all deals by the end of the month as promised. Although none of us would ever be the same, the gratitude that we all survived and were together again provided comfort and healing.

Commuting to Midtown was challenging. The closest subway available was at City Hall, which meant walking close to Ground Zero. The surrounding area was sectioned off but still close enough to see the pile, the still-smoking mountains of twisted steel, and mounds of debris. Close enough to hear a persistent beeping sound as you approached the perimeter of the site, a sound that faded after a few blocks. Each day I heard it. The chirping beep of a battery-powered device worn by firefighters and activated if a firefighter was motionless. The chirping bounced off the surrounding buildings and created a cacophony of sounds. It was a devastating scene.

It was during this time I learned how to evacuate the subway, if necessary, which lights meant what, and how to find an exit to the street from a tunnel. I carried a small "go pack" in my bag. It contained water, a mask, a flashlight, and a flare. My life was already well-adjusted to hypervigilance, and I easily added these skills. We soon moved into new offices and worked to rebuild our collective and individual professional and emotional lives. We were survivors now.

Many memories of the day live in my mind. Not so much the carnage itself, but the full parking lot at the ferry in the evening. The eerie silence of the streets and subways. The feeling of not wanting to smile or laugh. Understanding the bravery of the FDNY, NYPD, and all first responders who served and protected our city, along with civilians who stepped in to help. What lingers most are the photos. Hours after the attacks, they started to appear. Hundreds of photographs were taped to walls, streetlight poles, and fences, first within the perimeter of the site, then by the hospitals and major transit hubs in the city. The lost. The missing. The smiling faces of the people who simply went to work that morning with a short description of what color hair and eyes they had, what they might have been wearing, and what floor they worked on. Images from happy times of people who were loved. We see those same faces now, each year, in the photographs held in sorrowful hands on the anniversary of this hideous day, as their names are remembered, spoken, and echoed throughout Lower Manhattan.

As time moved on, I was able to tell this part of my personal story. In the first few years, it was hard to put words together to describe it. I was not injured physically. I was not in the building. I did not have to navigate forty flights of stairs to escape. I did not have to run for my life through a massive cloud of debris. What I did not understand until much later was the amount of emotional trauma I absorbed into an already-crowded space. As in any event of such life-altering proportion, it became a moment of changed perceptions and priorities.

The irony of *Gravity's Rainbow* was not lost on me. I never finished reading it. The bookmark remains stalled on page twenty-eight, the last words read before disaster struck and a screaming did come across the sky, a reference to Emily Dickinson:

Because I could not stop for Death
He kindly stopped for me

The words etched into the wall at the entrance to the 9/11 Memorial and Museum, on the grounds of the rebuilt World Trade Center complex, read, "No Day Shall Erase You From the Memory of Time."

The sorrowful complexity of that day lives eternally in my mind. Forgetting is not an option. The images are seared into my memory forever.

Today, I am reminded of how quickly the lessons were forgotten as we now, decades later, stand apart as a nation, divided and facing many threats, not from foreign extremists but from homegrown ones, incompetent leaders, and other watch-the-world-burn enthusiasts. The history of American efforts to force democracy in other lands seems to have only served to leave our own fragile idea of it in shambles. We need no outside help to tear ourselves down.

Chapter Seven

INTO THE THICK OF THINGS

Things changed after September 11. The graveness of the day, and all that surrounded it, was a stark reminder of the unpredictable and arbitrarily fragile lives we lead as humans. It shifted my entire perspective. It also caused my hidden secrets to stir. My close involvement in something so surreal and tragic pushed me toward taking a closer look at my life, where it had been, and where it was headed.

I made the decision to leave the band. The split ended badly and with much animosity. I lost a good deal of my gear, including a guitar I loved, a vintage-blond mid-1970s Fender Telecaster. Everything changed, and my life was moving forward in a new direction. The band had filled the void left by a fractured childhood and dysfunctional family life, and I was concerned that the rage I'd released over the past thirteen years through playing music would be directed inward again, having nowhere else to go. But my sitar studies gave me a new and different type of release. In the months following, I dove deeper into learning sitar and Indian classical music.

I went weekly for my lessons and cherished my time there

studying sitar with my teacher, an amazingly talented musician, woman, and mother. I was treated as a member of their family of greatly skilled players, who taught and performed throughout the city. Having them be a part of my life during this time was healing in many ways. The intricacy of Indian classical music required a type of devotion and loyalty I could not commit to beyond a few years as my life moved along. But it was the transition and the medicine I needed at the time to get me to the next phase of my path and remains close to my heart today.

As many people were thinking about leaving New York City, Mother returned, spurred by the events. Something changed in her when she thought I might not have survived the attacks. When she returned, she made more of an effort to be kind. Although the same awkward detachment we have always had remained, she was quick to say "please" and "thank you" when I took her grocery shopping or ran errands for her. For a time, I thought she had returned to try and repair our mother-daughter relationship. Maybe the events of September 11 had changed her perspective too and caused her to reflect. Good manners and basic civility were never her forte, but she was noticeably trying.

It did not last too long, but going forward she did manage to let it peek through occasionally as I reestablished my role as the helpful daughter.

However, my quiet and ever-present desperate quest to be seen as normal kept me steeped in comfortable lies. I continued to keep the secrets and carried the burdens of others, long after my childhood innocence was stolen from me. I gifted to a toxic family the secure illusion of normalcy by remaining silent. I kept them safe from the truth. My canopy of silence covered their deluge of failings like an umbrella in the rain. I had no healthy boundaries with Mother, a skilled manipulator who sucked from my wells of compassion, returning mere crumbs of approval.

As she aged, she wore the mask of a pitifully helpless old lady, like a fairy-tale witch who disguises herself as harmless, then devours those who come to her aid. Having been devalued, ravaged, and plundered as a child, I became a woman who had no boundaries, making sure everyone around me was comfortable even if I was not. I lived in a lifelong role reversal with Mother, where I provided her with mental and emotional support, leaving my own reserve empty. My quest for a loving connection, not as strong as in my childhood, remained, and my bullish Taurus nature kept coming back for more, trying repeatedly to improve our relationship. It was a fool's errand.

Mother told me she loved me. Once. On my wedding day. The words I had longed to hear as a child sounded like a foreign language I did not understand. It sounded like the words came dripping out in slow motion, and I wondered if she was directing the sentiment toward someone else. I did not know what to say. Did she speak the words solely for appearances' sake? For the benefit of anyone standing close enough to hear? But I had never loved her as an adult . . . as a child, I did, of course. I had wished for it to be reciprocated, but it just never was. My unending peacekeeping efforts led to inviting her to be part of this special day, but moments like that did not fit into our strange world.

There is not one picture of us together from the wedding. In her usual state of blankness, she sat on my wedding dress in the car, wrinkling it from the waist down. She was a constant thorn in my side and a perpetual burden to bear and never anything more. In this moment, I realized that the sooner I accepted it was too late for those words, the better off I was.

When Alex and I decided to start a family, stirrings of an unforeseen transition occurred, as the parched landscape of repressed and disregarded painful memories erupted. I had stopped smoking my medicine for the first time in twenty years. I hadn't been smoking in large quantities, just enough to get through the days distracted from reality. I was not high all the time, just leveled out, and I was still able to function quite well. Cannabis was the medicine I needed to keep myself safe. Once we decided to get pregnant, though, stopping this lifelong dependency was the first order of business.

My brain became well-defined for the first time in decades. It did not take long to notice the difference in being clearheaded as opposed to feeling perpetually clouded. I liked it, and at the same time, I did not. Clearheadedness felt like a foreign and dangerous place to be. As decades of my self-prescribed herbal-induced mental health protection lifted, so did the seal of what kept me safe from dreadful memories. But the thought of being a good mother took its place. I would do anything to be that.

Something cracked within me from the moment the plus sign appeared on the home pregnancy test on Christmas Eve morning. The memories I hid away started to stir and grow inside of me, alongside the baby I was bringing into this world. I was determined to ensure our child had everything I always longed for but never received. Not material possessions or financial riches, but, more importantly, love, emotional support, a sound moral compass, a good education, and above all safety and security.

Becoming a mother was a defining and transformative event for me. I realized much later that I mothered my wounded inner child in conjunction with mothering my baby from the moment of conception. I was not raised by role models who were skilled at parenting, but they did teach me something important in this area: what not to do.

After giving birth, the once-impenetrable seal on my secrets thinned. The memories and events I had long buried emerged more often than usual. The love I had for my baby was overwhelming, and his safety and happiness were my focus. I stared at him while he slept, watching him breathe for hours while my mind uncontrollably wandered into the thick of things. Staring at him dragged me into the past. His absolute innocence evoked my shattered one. I did not want to revisit those thoughts, but they were relentless. As they increasingly tried to pry their way out of confinement, shaking off a foggy history, they became distinct and unavoidable.

Twelve weeks later, I returned to work the second shift at the firm, arrangements I'd made prior to giving birth so we never needed to leave our child with a sitter or at a day care center. I did not possess the capacity for that level of trust. I slept when he slept during the day. It was exhausting, but his safety was all that mattered. My sweet little family became my new band, and I dedicated myself wholeheartedly to them, keeping the consistently taunting memories private and under tight lock and key.

Shortly after enrolling our child in a local Montessori preschool as a toddler, the financial crisis hit. I had been convinced this was positively the best start in life we could offer him, and if we carefully budgeted, we could find a way to afford it. Then came the worst economic disaster since the Great Depression of 1929. The firm was greatly affected. Our finance group was a key component to their overall prosperity and was deeply embedded in the crisis. After deals stalled and our major clients collapsed, the firm had no choice but to proceed with layoffs. After a few months, the firm went into dissolution. We survived September 11 but not this.

I received a fair severance package, which allowed us to continue our school payments and gave me time to look for another job. The government stepped in, the banks were bailed out, and their greed and reckless handling of the scenario that tanked our entire economy was treated as a gaffe. The bailouts made those responsible for the economic collapse rich again in no time.

I applied for and was hired at a local community-based health organization as an administrative assistant in their legal department. It was challenging, but I found my bearings quickly. I enjoyed being part of an important service to the community, and I took my work seriously. Our family grew a short time later when we welcomed our second child. We worked hard to provide a happy and healthy environment for our family.

After my maternity leave ended, the two executive-level positions I supported both resigned and were not immediately replaced. I worked diligently to keep our department in order. It was draining and demanding but offered a sense of pride and accomplishment. I thought it might earn me a promising future within the organization. Upon the advice of a colleague, I approached the director for her thoughts on a salary increase and title change.

Her first question to me was, "Where did you go to school?" I replied, "I didn't."

She was rude and smug. It seemed like she enjoyed telling me how I was not qualified for anything more than the administrative position. I explained to her that I'd been doing the jobs of two executives and a secretary upon my return from maternity leave for the last several months.

She responded, "Because of your lack of education, you do not qualify."

My body flooded with familiar shame, not only due to my lack of education being used against me so harshly but also because of everything that led to and was the reason behind it.

She did not evaluate me on my achievements or potential. She only saw my GED and no college education. She saw me as someone of a lower status than she was, and she elevated herself by excluding me. I was her subordinate, not her equal. She made sure I understood. She was accustomed to seeing through a normalized hierarchal lens. Instead of forming an opinion based on performance, she based it on whether I had a college education. If these old patterns of perceived roles in society continue to hold sway, they will only serve to push society backward instead of forward, with missed opportunities for employees and organizations. Coincidentally, in the days following this meeting, I received a call from a member of my team from the new firm they'd moved to after the dissolution and learned of an opportunity to come back. I accepted immediately.

My relationship with my children changed everything. Being a parent continually reminded me of how I was parented—or not parented, in my case. The love I held for them came naturally and was powerful. As they grew, I compared each related period of their lives to my own. Things started to become clear. This was when and how I realized and faced the extent of the lack of care and love I experienced and the damage I was subjected to because of it.

The mother-child bond is the purest love there is, but when it is steeped in abuse, secrets, trauma, and fear, it is the darkest and most harsh loss a child can ever experience. How I disregarded it with a smile on my face was even sadder.

The fractures in my memory were affecting not just my mental health but my physical health as well. I experienced episodes of chronic pelvic pain. After many medical visits, MRIs, and exams, my doctors did not have an answer. The costly tests provided no clear diagnosis or resolution besides the recommendation for unnecessary surgeries and prescription pills.

The pain was intense and would appear out of nowhere with no warning. Every few months, usually at the most inopportune time, like while I was at work or commuting, I was thrust into severe and debilitating pelvic pain.

In hindsight, it was the truth, the trauma, and the pain bubbling to the surface, demanding to be set free. Each bout of pain brought the truth closer to my lips and took over my thoughts.

I did not know how much longer I could hold it in. The veneer covering my traumatic secrets became unstable. The truth was fracturing my whole being. It woke me in the middle of the night. It was there in a sound, a song, or when my children surprised me from behind. It was there through the seasons and the temperature outside. It was there through certain smells. It lurked in the shadows on the wall. It was always there, waiting to pounce.

When my oldest child was eight years old, the approximate age of my first clear memory of being abused, the recollections refused my usual silencing techniques and kept surfacing. I had intense flashbacks of sitting on the chair in the middle of the living room. Paula and Carol from *The Magic Garden* gently sang while strumming their acoustic guitars on the television while I tapped along on the thick cover of the heavy encyclopedia.

When I closed my eyes at night, I was sitting on that couch. I could almost feel the scratchy material on my legs and hear the laughter from the group of boys, the one from upstairs telling them to leave. I could see him in my mind closing each of the shades on the four windows slowly, one by one, darkening the room and trapping me. *We are finally alone.* There were also other memorialized events and random vivid images of terrible scenes I had no memory of but that started to appear in my dreams.

The historically impenetrable and hard outer layer of survival armor I wore was compromised for the first time. It was worn, cracking, and splitting open, and I was nearly bursting out of it. My ability to bury memories and forget, even if only temporarily, and long enough to find a distraction, was gone. The unplanned yet inevitable release of truth, albeit partially, came stampeding out at the end of a routine day. All the rage and pain simmering beneath the surface could not be contained any longer. I gagged on its wretchedness. It was me versus the secrets of trauma since childhood, and, for the first time, I lost.

It was at the end of a long, hot summer day of outdoor activity when my pin got snagged and I exploded. I was exhausted, cleaning up before bed, when Alex said something to me. I do not recall his exact words. It could have simply been, "Do you need help?" The explosion was unplanned and intense. It took thirty-six years for me to burst and reveal what had happened that day, with the teenage boy, the mice, the couch, but, finally, I spoke those words aloud. He was shocked . . . just as shocked as I was to hear those words come out of my mouth.

Decades of tears poured from my eyes, and my body shook uncontrollably as I tried my best to keep my screams soft and muffled by a pillow. I could not find the words yet to continue with the other truths I held: The Priests, the cover-up, my descent into despair, the drug use, and the attempted suicide. They, too, were banging on my lips, trying to force them open so they could also be released from their long captivity, but I was not ready for it all. Neither was Alex, but the seal had been broken. One step at a time.

This was the start of the unloading of vile burdens I had carried and concealed all my life. I felt a great deal of relief after those words were spoken, even if it was not the whole story. But I did not have the luxury of wallowing in a breakdown—I had a life I had to continuously function in—nor would I ever let our children see me compromised. We gradually talked about what happened a little at a time.

One year later, I unexpectedly exploded again, this time with an even higher sense of urgency. It happened as we watched and listened to Michelle Obama's speech in Manchester, New Hampshire, supporting a Hilary Clinton campaign event on October 13, 2016.[5] The power and persuasion of her eloquent and compassionate words opened the next fissure in my body. Words describing a candidate who so easily demeaned and bragged about smearing and sexually assaulting women to cheering crowds struck me and widened the existing fracture from my first disclosure. My heart rate steadily increased as she spoke. I tensed as she described how it shook her to her core to witness this unbelievable display of repulsive behavior. How it was not something she could ignore, how disturbed she was, and how she tried to shield her daughters from the obscene language and actions we all witnessed, much like I did with my children.

My breathing became labored when she said, "and the truth is, it hurts." The words were fading in and out: "a little too close, stares a little too long. . . . It's that feeling of terror and violation that too many women have felt when someone has grabbed them, or forced himself on them and they've said no but he didn't listen."

I stood and walked quickly out of the room. I could not hear any more.

The still-undisclosed parts of my truth were bubbling to the surface, ready to race from my lips. I was choking on them. As I made my way to the bathroom, more of her words seeped in "this kind of violence and abuse and disrespect . . . We are drowning in it. . . . doing what women have always done . . . trying to get through it. . . . Maybe we've grown accustomed to swallowing these emotions and staying quiet, because we've seen that people often won't take our word over his. Or maybe we don't want to believe that there are still people out there who think so little of us as women . . . as if our outrage is overblown or unwarranted."

I closed the door to my bedroom and sobbed. I knew I needed to take the next step of telling the rest of my story.

The next morning, I confessed to Alex. "I did not tell you everything last year," I said, "only some of it. There is more. I was sexually assaulted by a priest at school. It may have been two priests, sometime between the fifth and sixth grade."

Alex was again shocked and horrified. So was I.

Over the next few weeks, I stepped onto the path of what would become a long and winding healing journey, one with as many benefits as bumps in the road to navigate. There was no turning back. My exposed secrets swirled around me in memories, images, and emotions. Bringing awareness to my repressed memories was startling and scary but carried huge benefits. Each word I spoke released the weight I had been carrying. It was gut-wrenching for me to speak about the challenges I faced as child. Saying "attempted suicide" out loud for the first time was surreal.

Only by embracing the truth of your past can you be free of pain in the present.

The truth slowly crept out of my bones and throughout my body to make its way to my lips. I was heard by someone who loved me. Over the next few months, each piece of the story was gently told. I was sad, yet relieved, to give voice to these hidden words, removing the remains of the once–tightly fitted mask, which had been slipping off slowly over the last decade.

During this time, my relationship with Mother, already endlessly compromised, wound down to limited contact. My initial thought was to confront her and demand the truth, but I knew she would call me a liar and tell me I was making up stories. I could not risk that hurt and decided the best approach would be to back off. She was never going to be the mother I needed and deserved, and it was time for me to accept it and focus on healing my wounds.

Over the following winter, my truth telling led to a quest to understand how trauma affects the mind and body of a child, and how the psychological harm of shame and secret keeping disturbs maturation. The first book I read was *The Body Keeps the Score: Brain, Mind, and Body in the Healing of Trauma*, by Bessel van der Kolk. This book was a transformative experience because it helped me to understand the complex psychological, neurobiological, and developmental effects of trauma. It also led me to discover the important work of Gabor Maté, Peter Levine, and more whose writings on trauma, stress, and childhood development helped me to examine my history from its roots through an informed and compassionate lens.

I spent a lot of time thinking about my childhood and allowed myself to remember the traumatic encounters . . . but this time through the lens of an adult. I sadly realized an unsaid pact endured within my family to keep quiet about dysfunction. This history of manipulated silence attributed to my muzzled lips. I had gone along with the plan . . . until now. I felt a strange mix of fear and delight.

Trauma-based emotions held me back from realizing my true self and what I could achieve. They kept me from receiving a complete education and the opportunities that might have followed. I did as well as I could have, and allowed myself to be proud, but had lost so much. Trauma, fear, and shame are powerful forces, and they were used to manipulate me and bend me toward others' wills. These emotions depend on secrecy to thrive and were my perceived inescapable prison bars. As soon as my secrets were revealed, they lost their power.

I could have ended up in a much different situation. What would have happened to me if I did not find and pursue my love of music, which saved me and led me to all that serendipitously followed?

I learned how when children feel shame, they do not think about the involvement of others and their indecent acts or behaviors being wrong; they think there is something implicitly wrong with them. It made sense to me. Feelings of discomfort and disconnection were pervasive throughout my life. It was why I never felt like I belonged.

When the root causes of traumatic events are kept hidden, they fester and cause permanent darkness, which blocks you from fully experiencing the richness of life and all it has to offer. The earlier in life trauma and the related concealment are burdened upon you, the more difficult they are to overcome. As children, we submit to the will of our authority figures . . . first parents, who are our lifeline and needed for our immediate and basic care, followed by aunts, uncles, grandparents, elders, teachers, etc. As we embrace the requirements of others, these relationships influence a distortion of our true selves. Often the actions of others are rooted in personal pain, rage, and destructive behaviors, which are redirected toward you. These events and experiences create repressed memories within a system that functions by keeping not only you but others in ignorance. This keeps you unconscious and is designed to perpetuate fear and control amid thoughts of not being believed. Fear breeds fear. Secrets breed secrets and cause a lack of social connection and a feeling of living in isolation. Consumed by an obsession with keeping secrets hidden is like endlessly carrying around a backpack full of heavy rocks.

The year following the second phase of my truth telling, the Me Too movement burst onto the scene. The timing was impeccable. The framework of the movement was originally used on social media in 2006 by activist Tarana Burke. But it was now thrust into the spotlight under celebrity influence as an empowerment tool and social justice movement following the rape and sexual assault allegations filed against film producer, Harvey Weinstein.

My quest for knowledge about these subjects became obsessive. I listened to podcasts or read on my morning and evening commutes. The chronic pelvic pain, which surfaced every few months with no clear diagnosis, lessened when I addressed the pain of my trauma. I started to make the connection. First, I learned to breathe. Long inhales and even longer exhales with spacing in between. Yogic deep-breathing techniques release accumulated tension, anxiety, and stress. Breathing deeply felt foreign, and I thought I must have never taken a deep breath before because I lived in a perpetual state of PTSD. Rapid, shallow breathing and tense muscles felt normal to me.

I started to go backward, reviewing my life year after year. I felt suffocated while exploring the details of what happened to me. Sometimes I wanted to go back to pretending everything was fine. I knew I had to encourage this new and truthful part of my voice to continue to speak. My attempt at mitigating traumatic and harmful memories and freeing myself from their restraints launched a journey of self-discovery.

I understood how I over-functioned in life to create a sense of normalcy and spent much of my time in a state of ignorance because it was much easier to digest.

Ignorance is bliss until it becomes clear it is just pure ignorance. Avoiding the demanding and difficult parts of life is what stunts growth and prevents us from moving forward. Denial is harmful and lives inside of our bodies alongside the underlying cause, and it is likely the truth will come, at some point, bursting out. Knowledge is bliss, not ignorance. It is resilient; it is personal power. Knowledge will set you free. What was the absolute truth I needed to tell myself? How would I cope by acknowledging the truth? How would I move forward?

In the pursuit of truth and healing, I examined certain puzzling traits I held, like the immediate anxiety that flooded me every time I sat in the back seat of a car or swam in a pool. If I drove through my old neighborhood, I would feel sick to my stomach. My brain thought these traits and reactions were ridiculous, but my body was telling me another story. I needed to understand why I was having these reactions. I needed answers.

The effects of trauma, which never once left my thoughts, combined with a complete lack of acknowledgment or help almost ended my life at just fourteen years old. The weight of trauma from extreme to minor and the subtle aftershocks growing one into another formed a feeling of there being no way back from those experiences.

Childhood sexual abuse is soul murder. It is a tragic, life-altering event, and it leaves a lasting, guttural pain and a unique rage engraved into the body, mind, and soul. This pain is strong enough to jeopardize the continuance of life and is a sadness I know thoroughly.

I was not able to look at myself in a mirror, into my own eyes, until I acknowledged and accepted the truths of my life. I did not look myself squarely in the eyes until I was forty-four years old. Instead, I wore the scarlet letter that had been pinned to my innocent flesh for too long . . . this was what shame did.

It was not Medusa's evil glare that turned men to stone; it was the truth of her story, which emanated from her eyes. Her stare told the story of her rape by Poseidon in the temple of Athena. She, like many victims of sexual assault, was vilified to carry out the sentence of the evil deeds of her abusers, becoming a demon herself, which conveyed the impression of rape being the victim's fault. The venomous snakes she wore as her hair held the venom of truth. The hearts of those who tried to exert power over her were already made of stone before her truthful gaze caused their whole being to follow.

Because we cannot look her straight in the eye, she dares us to look inward, to face the authenticity of our unspoken truth.

To look inward and face my truth, I first needed to know exactly what my truth was. Until now, it had been something too painful to face, elusive and unreachable, but if I was going to regain my true self, my purpose, and my power, I had to find it.

Chapter Eight

FLIPPING THE SWITCH

"Flipping the switch" is a metaphor used to describe the act of making a change from one position to its precise opposite. Flipping to the "on" position changes a space from a state of darkness to a state of light. A sense of powerlessness can be felt when we cannot find the switch in a darkened room. Brushing a hand across walls closest to an entryway or other areas where you think a switch might be located while blinded by darkness causes the heightening of other senses to balance the loss of sight. Light organizes visual perception, provides a sense of security and power within the environment, and gives us the ability to navigate surroundings easily and fluidly. But what if you can't easily find the switch? Do you continue the search, or do you resign yourself to the dimness?

I sat in a small windowless room with soft lighting reflecting off lavender walls. A miniature fountain in the corner gave the calming sound of falling water and combined with a light fragrance of incense, creating a serene and soothing ambiance. As I sat in one of the soft chairs, I thought about how I was about to divulge lifelong secrets to someone I had never even met before.

I was nervous, but it was time for me to move forward in sincere transparency. I knew I needed help navigating this new world of truth telling, but traditional talk therapy did not feel like the right fit for me. I needed guidance to go deeper to tolerate the wounds I had unleashed and fully address my past.

Even Michele did not know my deepest secrets. She and I have always been linked in a way that benefited both of us through introducing shared interests. I was grateful we mended our friendship after September 11. One day, she casually mentioned she had recently met someone who practiced Reiki. I had been curious about Reiki, as it had popped up in different ways over the last few years. It immediately seemed like a good way to get started on the inner work I knew I had to do. I searched online within the local area and found Jean Bromage, a seasoned Reiki master. When I saw her photo, I knew she was the right person.

Reiki is a form of energy healing that was developed by Usui Mikao, a Japanese spiritual seeker, in the early 1920s. Through his search for awakening, or *satori*, he discovered the ability to become a conduit for an energy flow that held healing properties.[6] After many years of study, he developed the Usui Reiki Ryoho, or Usui Reiki Healing Method, a hands-on healing practice whereby the practitioner becomes the conduit for Reiki energy to flow into themselves for self-healing or through themselves to another recipient. Reiki is an accessible, versatile practice and can be learned by anyone. It causes no harm and needs no special tools. The benefits are vast, and today the practice of Reiki is increasingly being accepted in the medical community as a beneficial, drug-free method of healing. Although I tried to learn a little about Reiki before my appointment, I did not know what to expect; I only knew I needed help.

I waited just a short time before Jean opened the door to the adjacent room. A calm comfort and a sense I had made the right decision embraced me. Connecting with Jean and Reiki served as the catalyst to completely reframing my entire life—past, present, and future, within and without.

The session started with basic introductions and a conversation about why I was interested in Reiki and what I hoped to gain from the experience. It was hard to get the words out initially, but as I continued talking, the words came surprisingly easy. I told Jean I experienced childhood trauma, including sexual abuse and the resulting self-abuse that continued throughout my younger years, and how I had never been to a therapist and thought this would be a good place for me to start. I explained how I had held on to these experiences for more than three decades without telling anyone.

Seated in comfortable chairs in front of a large window that looked out over the bustle of the city, Jean listened intently as I traveled this new road of disclosing words long unspoken. It was as if a supportive hand were on my back bracing me against their weight. I felt safe revealing these secrets in this space. After our conversation, we moved to the hands-on healing part of the session.

Jean described Reiki as the spiritual energy within everything that exists. Coupling with this energy returned you to the heart of your true essence. Within this flow of energy, in the presence of divine grace and unconditional love, one can experience a quieting of the mind, a calming of the heart, and a restoration of overall well-being.

Jean further described Reiki as "the white canvas upon which all of life paints itself."

I lay back on the table and closed my eyes. I tried to relax my ever-spinning mind. Jean explained each phase of the session as she went along. Soft, relaxing music played as she placed crystals around my body, on my heart, and one in each hand. She hovered her hands just above the top of my head. After a few minutes, I felt a warmth radiating from them.

As she moved to the next hand position on the sides of my head, I felt a deep relaxation of my neck and shoulder muscles. Surprisingly, scores of tears streamed from my eyes, but I was not crying. The tears were effortlessly flowing. As much as my mind started racing to make sense of what was happening, I took a breath and allowed myself to understand how those effortless tears were the gentle release of decades' worth of held sorrows. It was a massive purge of the deep sadness I'd held in secret for so long.

As Jean continued, I felt tingling in the areas of my body that she addressed. It was strongest when she moved to my hips. She explained how we hold trauma, old emotions, and unconscious tension in the pelvic area, which causes a tightening and compression in the hips. This was true for all types of traumas and stress, but none more than sexual trauma. Jean explained that the tension released that day could stir up emotions I may not expect. She reminded me to find the deepest self-compassion as they arose.

Over an hour went by in what felt like minutes. As the session came to an end, Jean recommended taking a few moments before sitting up. I felt my loosened limbs and muscles. For the first time in my life, I felt my body in a way I had never perceived it before. I had been living in a tense and constricted body. As I sat up, turned, and slid off the table, I felt refreshed and relaxed. Jean recommended some books I could read to learn more about Reiki and healing in general. She reminded me to give myself time to settle into the newness of speaking the truth and the changes taking place in my mind, body, and soul.

Before leaving, Jean asked me to pick a mantra from a list of uplifting quotes and sentiments I could use as I processed the experience over the next few days. I chose "I am a radiant being, filled with light and love." It was perfect because it was exactly how I felt. Jean was reusing the back blank pages from an old calendar and wrote the statement on the paper for me. I told her before she turned it over to reveal the date on the calendar that it would be funny if it was number eleven, since that number has followed me for decades.

She said, "That's a magical number." She turned it over. Wednesday, the eleventh!

Throughout the days playing in the band, the number eleven followed Michele and me everywhere, separately and together. We finished rehearsing and checked the time: 11:11. We had a gig and were ready to go onstage: 11:11. We headed out to grab lunch in the afternoon: 1:11. The order was number eleven. We laughed but did not pay close enough attention. After my session, it had my full attention.

I had undergone LASIK eye surgery a few years prior to correct my vision. The surgery was painless and quick, and when it was over the doctor told me to look at a clock on the wall quite a distance away.

Out of habit, I grabbed for my glasses, and the doctor said, "You won't need them anymore."

I looked across the room and stared at the clock. "It is ten o'clock! I can see it!" I could not believe I could see without my glasses. My lifelong dependence on corrective eyewear was over.

Leaving Jean's office after my Reiki session felt like my experience with LASIK surgery. I stepped out of the building onto Madison Avenue and stood on the sidewalk, noticing how everything looked different. Everything was crystal clear; even the hectic noise of cars and people, which usually sounded obnoxiously loud, was softened. I blinked repeatedly, noticing the clarity in my vision. I could not make sense of it. As I headed to the corner to cross the street and return to work, it seemed like everything was shining: the buildings, the people, the street, and the sky.

I walked slowly, processing what had happened. Something deep within me had shifted. A voice in my head said, *You must leave here.* If I wanted to go on this journey wholeheartedly and find the life I was meant to lead, I needed to leave New York City. The voice was my inner voice, my intuition, the part of me that was connected to *all* and knew the way. It was my higher self, coming from deep within. It was not the voice of ego, which would be the voice of the physical, the collective, and the external.

On the heels of my session with Jean, and after decades of silence, I found the switch that activated the brightest of lights within my heart. This light would help me see clearly while I dug around in the darkness of shadowed memories. After a lifetime of living in the dimness, I chose to step fully into the light of truth and onto the road of what would become an intense healing journey. It was time.

As music had been the catalyst that saved my life in my younger years, the discovery of energy medicine in the form of Reiki appeared precisely when I was ready to receive it. I knew I had no choice but to follow my instincts about leaving New York City. It also became clear, without hesitation, that Vermont was the best place for me and my family to relocate to. I had never been to Vermont and had known only one person from there. I had long admired the progressiveness of the state, but whatever the reason behind my clarity, I had a deep knowing it was the right place. I was being guided there, and if I did not listen and act on this guidance, I would regret it for the rest of my life. As the nation was stepping onto a journey of impending doom that likely would not end well, I was stepping onto the path of my own long-awaited journey.

Things were altered in a way I could not yet fully define. I felt different in many ways. I viewed my past as an open wound that needed to be cleansed and covered to heal the infection of trauma. I also noticed feelings in my body I had not had before. Like whenever I was in Mother's company, I felt incredibly nauseous, and once she and I were apart, I was fine. What was my body telling me?

I shed my usual people-pleaser syndrome and spoke up more easily. I was bursting at the seams and on the precipice of encountering something grand. It was thrilling and exciting but also daunting. My breathing was deeper, and I had a lightness in my body. I'd always had the feeling I was not doing something I was supposed to be doing. It had been a whisper in my ear. Now, until I acted on putting in place the essential changes, the whisper became a scream.

Over the last twenty years, I had spent a lot of time reading about esoteric subjects, pondering the matters of the universe, the soul, meditation, death, and reincarnation. My search for spirituality brought me to Eastern philosophies in my early twenties. I read many books on these and related subjects. I sensed a relationship to higher planes of thought and was on a constant hunt for information. All the reading and contemplating prepared my understanding and open-mindedness to energy medicine but would never provide the true emotional connection I'd searched for until I spoke my truth. Only when I was honest with myself and faced my wounds head-on would the connection happen. I was stepping into my true self as it materialized; it was startling and invigorating. If I continued to live in shame and secrecy, lying to myself and those closest to me, my life, although certainly not dull, would not be all it was meant to be.

Each day on my way to work in the morning or at lunchtime, I stopped at the Midtown Manhattan library to pick up or return book after book on Reiki, healing, and energy medicine. The selection on these subjects was vast, and I devoured as much information as I could find.

Reiki quickly became a profound and integral part of my life. This work carved a path forward and gifted me a beautiful release of long-held pain and grief. It awakened my body, mind, and spirit in a pure form that had been unreachable before. The outside world looked different, and my inside world shifted. The heavy weight of the burdens I carried for so long eased. I knew I needed to learn more about Reiki, and Jean was the perfect teacher.

I completed Reiki Level I (Shoden) early the following year in a small class expertly led by Jean. We covered the history of Reiki, the related elements of Buddhism and Shinto, the importance of breathing exercises as a form of meditation, and more. We learned the hand positions and how they directed the flow of energy through body anatomy, the chakra system, and the meridians. It was an intense and in-depth training. Becoming attuned to the Reiki System of Natural Healing resulted in becoming a conduit or transmitter of the spiritual or transcendent life force energy, allowing it to flow through us to a person, animal, or any object, animate or inanimate. As observers, we stood in stillness in the center of the energy flow.

I was fascinated with every aspect. What a different world it would be if this were accessible to everyone. My experiences with Reiki and how it worked created a constant question and dialogue in my mind: *What is energy? How are we as humans capable of channeling it? Are we able to heal ourselves?*

I spent time examining and exploring the world of energy and healing and completed Reiki Level II (Okuden) a few months later. In this class, Jean covered distance healing techniques, which included learning to send or transmit energy to another person in a separate space. After learning the preparation and transmission techniques, we split into pairs, with one group remaining in the room and the other moving into an adjacent room. Jean led us through each part of the session, and when we finished and called in the group who'd left the room, the expression on their faces was amazement. We switched positions, and my group left the room. We sat quietly and waited. I felt the energy, first in the bottom of my feet, then up my legs, through my torso, up my back, and to the back of my neck. My partner was transmitting the energy to me from the opposite room, just as I had done for her. I was completely awestruck.

Included in my next pick of books at the library was *Quantum Physics for Dummies*. I did not understand any of it. I went on to read in snippets about what Einstein called "spooky action at a distance."[7] In 1964, physicist John Bell proved what Einstein had found "spooky" was indeed real.[8]

Bell's theorem used entanglement to show how two distinct particles can lose their independence the moment they are measured, and how the result of one instantly affects the outcome of the other regardless of the distance between them. Tap a particle here, and its partner will be affected, immediately, no matter how far away the second particle is.

Although I wanted to understand this work in a more complete way, I knew with time it would come. It was more important to continue learning in an experiential and first-hand manner, finding the ability to connect emotionally and spiritually with energy. Trying to understand the magnitude of the relationship between science and energy medicine was causing stagnation. I knew enough to proceed not just on faith alone, of which I had a limited supply, and would revisit the scientific connection as time went on. It was impossible to be skeptical about what I had experienced thus far.

In addition to Reiki, Jean also practiced shamanism, a subject I had become interested in through my obsession with The Doors and Jim Morrison's poetry many years earlier. I picked up a book recommended by Jean, *Awakening to the Spirit World*, by Sandra Ingerman and Hank Wesselman. While reading this book, I experienced a spontaneous shamanic encounter.

It was early summer. In the middle of the night, I had what I thought was a lucid dream. It seemed as if I was awake but dreaming at the same time. I was following a "being" through a winding tunnel; the being kept turning and motioning for me to follow. I followed through many twists and turns before there was a break in the tunnel. The being crawled through an opening to enter another passageway. I did not follow because I was scared and backed off. My body stretched out on a patch of grass on the side of a creek. I could feel and smell the grass beneath me. I heard rushing water and felt a light mist of spray on my face.

I was still not sure if I was awake or dreaming. I smelled the scents of water, flowers, grass, and trees. I attempted to open my eyes when I sensed a presence in the room. I was frightened and squeezed my eyes shut. All my senses were heightened. My heart was beating fast, and my whole body tingled with the familiar flow of energy. I knew if I opened my eyes, someone or something was going to be standing there. I slowly pulled the blankets over my head. The feeling, the smells, and the sounds instantly left. I stayed under the covers a bit longer.

When I finally peeked out, the room was dark except for the faint light of the nearest streetlight. The air conditioner was humming; my rational brain took over and I wondered if that was the streaming-water sound I had mistaken for a creek. But I didn't think so. I felt like a kid, afraid of a monster under the bed.

It was easy to think I was going crazy. The rational part of my brain immediately intervened to make it seem that way. These thoughts were quieted quickly though. I was fully aware of what I was experiencing.

The oddness continued in small occurrences and in synchronicities I could not disregard. I heard my name spoken clearly in my head one summer evening while in the backyard tidying up. It was clear yet gentle and soft. I felt a presence near the right side of my body. Everything I'd learned over the last twenty years was absorbed in a logical sense. Mounds of information swirled in my head and became clear in a different way. The normally blocked emotional connection through my heart was softening. I was not just soaking up knowledge through my brain; I was engaging with it and understanding it through a deeply intuitive awareness in my heart.

Around this time, I had a note on my dresser with a reminder to find a rose quartz crystal to keep in my pocket to assist in maintaining the work of healing and opening my heart. Rose quartz held significance with a connection to my name and ancestral history. It dispelled negativity and replaced it with love. It was calming and opened the heart to support inner healing. I made it my mission to find the perfect one.

As summer was fading and fall was on the horizon, I spent time cleaning out our linen closet and replacing summer sheets with winter blankets in preparation for the cooler weather. As I removed a set of folded sheets, I found a plastic bag on the shelf behind them. It contained small gifts given to me by a friend who visited from South America the prior year. I must have stuck it in there and forgotten all about it. I pulled out a pretty hair clip and a small neck scarf. A heavy item was at the bottom. I walked toward the window to get a good look at it, away from the faint light of the hallway. The sunlight revealed a beautiful rose quartz. It glistened in the palm of my hand. A familiar rush of energy climbed up my legs and into my back. I held the crystal to my heart and felt its warmth against my chest. I whispered, "Thank you."

Throughout the fall and winter, there were times when I felt like I was suffocating. The city streets, which once energized me, were doing the exact opposite now. During my long daily commute to and from work, I felt like I was carrying an elephant on my back.

When things, people, or places in your life are not in your best interest, you can feel it in your gut and have a clear and unavoidable knowing. You must act, or those choking feelings will keep reminding you. They will grab and shake you until you listen.

There were only two choices: listen to the guidance and create a new life, or shut it off and go back to the familiar life I led, undoubtedly not perfect, authentic, or truthful, but not terrible. It was not just my life, but also my family as individuals I needed to consider. I knew the answer. We held hands and jumped off the cliff together.

We visited Vermont in early spring. I had a feeling of being at home in a place I had never been to before. Thankfully, my family agreed, and a few months later, we packed and headed north for a new life.

Before leaving for Vermont, I met my oldest friends, Cissy, May, and Annalyn, at a restaurant in the neighborhood where we all grew up. We had all attended St. Paul's together. I now lived just a mile away but rarely drove through the area. After dinner, I walked home for one last look at the places that bore witness to my childhood secrets. I walked slowly past our old apartment building. Everything looked the same. Being there stirred the memories that were slowly becoming clearer in my mind, the secrets that were no longer secrets. The darkness around my memories was thinning. I stopped at the corner and stared down the dead-end street where I had played with friends from early in the morning until the streetlights came on, riding borrowed bikes and making crayon-wax-bottle mandalas. I wondered if their lives were as perfect as I thought them to be, or if they hid secrets too. I crossed the street and walked along the same route I'd once used to get to school.

I strolled slowly, taking it all in, remembering details as quick flashes of images and memories inundated my head. I stood in the spot where the dog attacked and remembered the scratchy wool coat sleeve covered with its saliva. As I approached St. Paul's, I stopped in front of the rectory at the back of the school. It looked the same. I stared at the screen door on the side of the house. My heartbeat increased. My body was responding.

Being there in person intensified the clarity of my memories. Although it was a sunny summer evening leaning toward dusk, the rectory was surrounded by a grayish haze. I stood there for a long time. I needed to remember. I saw no movement inside or outside; no light came from the windows as twilight set in. I looked over at the large gold cross affixed to the back of the school building diagonally across from the screen door. I wondered how many other kids had stood and stared at that cross, certain I was not the only one.

Chapter Nine

WAKING UP IN VERMONT

There is an old fable about a cracked pot that teaches how our lives are shaped by the stories we tell ourselves about who we are:

A woman walked a long way every morning to a creek to collect water in two pots hanging from a pole she carried across her shoulders. One pot was in perfect condition; the other had a crack in its side, and by the time the woman returned home, it was only ever half full.

As the years passed by, the cracked pot created a story in its head about its worthiness and inability to fulfill the important job of carrying water. Eventually, the shame it felt about its imperfections became too much for it to bear. One day, as the woman knelt beside the river to fill the pots, the cracked pot found its voice.

"For years you have filled me with water, and I can only wonder about your frustration," it said. "Whenever we return home, I am only ever half full. The other pot is perfect; it does not lose a drop of water on our long walk back home. I am far from perfect. This crack in my side, not only does it cause me so much shame, but it must also cause you to want to get rid of me. I am surely only making this daily task much more difficult for you. I will understand if you want to get rid of me and replace me with a new, perfectly formed pot."

The woman listened with compassion. She knew about the crack but did not see it as an imperfection. She kindly said, "On our walk home, I want you to look up. For too long, you have been looking down, comparing yourself to others and not noticing how you and your perceived imperfection have brought much beauty into my life."

On the return journey, the pot looked up and saw how the path they walked along was filled with a beautiful array of magnificent wildflowers. The woman, knowing of the crack in the pot's side, had sprinkled seeds along the path. As a result of the crack in the pot, the seeds were duly watered every day.

The cracked pot saw itself in a new light. The pot understood it had been telling itself a cruel and wounding story. If the pot's point of view was going to change, then it would have to change the story it was telling itself and look up to see the beauty it helped to create.

Although it was still a melancholy time, leaving New York City was not difficult. The dizzying excitement of forging a new path lay ahead. Vermont was the place I needed to heal, a peaceful environment to do my healing work, allowing me space to breathe away from the crowds, congestion, and drudgery of long commutes.

If Dante's *Divine Comedy* had a tenth layer of hell, it would consist of performing the routine of my daily commute in a loop forever, the purgatorial slog of cramming into small spaces with excessive amounts of people on all matters of transport. It was surely the one tedious chore I would not miss. Yes, it has its romanticized version, but that is mostly for tourists.

After twenty years, I had reached my personal cutoff. I have had many interesting ferry and subway rides and acquired important skills like the ability to successfully read a book while in the presence of a dozen different conversations, leaked music from headphones, and the mumble of the conductor over the sound of the train rumbling through the tracks. I would miss the cultural experiences of the city, but enjoying those experiences became limited after having a family due to the extravagant cost of living there.

For the first few months after arriving in Vermont, I often dreamed of the city. Most were anxiety-driven dreams in the vein of my kids being left alone in a random place like Union Square Park in the middle of the night while I was on Forty-Second Street, shoeless and frantically trying to get to them. I often dreamed of being in our studio in the Music Building. The space felt so real. The outside light reflected off the walls and windows, with intermittent sounds of music and sirens in the background. As I slept on the couch, a loud noise woke me. I looked out the window and down to the street. A gigantic tiger blocked traffic, roaring at the cars and pedestrians, who screamed and ran away. The tiger was not attacking, just stomping with its giant paws, baring large sharp teeth. I was not scared. I knew if I was in our studio, I was safe.

The tiger showed up in my dream to awaken the strength I would need to move forward as I embraced a new and very different way of life. As I unearthed emotional wounds and searched for truth, the tiger represented courage and a reminder to embrace my intuition, instincts, and feminine energy. My life in the band and the countless hours spent in our studio were the foundation of my healing journey, where I found safety and personal growth and what had prepared me for this moment. The tiger finds solitude in the jungle; I would find it in the forests of Vermont.

Verd Mont (Green Mountain) was the name given to this land by Samuel de Champlain in 1647; it became Vermont around

1760. Vermont was admitted to the union as the fourteenth state in 1791, the year of my birth backward. This land was the traditional territory of the Abenaki people, who lived for generations in harmony with its bounty. We settled near the beauty and magic of Lake Champlain. This was where my healing work would take place. This was where I came to find my purpose.

There is a strong correlation between healing and connection to the natural world. Spending time in nature has a robust effect on aiding our physical, mental, and emotional health. Nature is vital to human life; it calms the nervous system and cultivates positive emotions. Living near green spaces provides a quiet atmosphere, beautiful scenery, and clean air. Towering trees attune us to things larger, not just in stature. They are nature's antennae connecting the earth and the divine. The forest is sacred, alive, and conversant. We can experience feelings of connection with other living things, the chirping of birds, and the flurry of activity of small forest creatures. We can experience the connection to the elements of nature in the seasons, the feel of a breeze on our faces, the smell of fresh rain, and the beauty of falling snow. Nature provides resources, life sustenance, and medicine. Being in balance with this bounty teaches us to be gentle and encourages care for the earth, for ourselves, and for others. Humanity's relationship to nature has not always been with reverence, and we are clearly seeing the damage we have caused to our own peril.

It took time for me to be comfortable with being in nature alone. I lived on high alert, with fear sewn into my pocket, and being in the forest was no different from being in the city. I understood how trauma left its mark of unease by inspecting my own emotions and actions closely. I started slowly, spending just a few minutes at a time, becoming more comfortable with each visit. With my sweet Labrador, my brave companion forging the path farther each time we visited, I became more at ease. I could see the smile on her face as we entered the trail. She was happy in the forest, with so many scents to sniff along the winding paths. Her eyes darted between squirrels scaling trees and scurrying chipmunks. She had no other mission, no worries about the future or regrets about the past. As we walked through the forest together, I organized my thoughts and memories. Taking notes in my journal, I started from the beginning with the basics.

How do you find your true self when you only have information based on lies and repressed and altered memories? Neither Mother nor anyone else ever thought facts or details on any topic were important, and I had always thought there was so much I did not know. I had never met anyone from Father's side of the family; I was always curious about them. Now that I was on a mission to make peace with my past, I had to understand my family history. Growing up, I was told my heritage was Italian and Irish, a clean fifty-fifty split. I knew this was not the whole story and started there.

I ordered a DNA test from Ancestry. My results, as expected, told a much different story. I am mostly Italian, followed by Scottish, with small, even percentages of French and Welsh. Finding out this information was a validation of what I already knew. I signed up for a membership account where I was able to search the database and gather information for a family tree.

A plan effortlessly formed in my head. My proposed strategy was not one of revenge or retribution, but one of validation and truth. The first step I took was to contact St. Paul's to request my records. I did not expect the details of my abuse to be memorialized in writing, but perhaps there would be helpful information about my tuition payments or other clues. I was ready to speak my truth and, somehow, have the satisfaction of fair and legitimate justice.

When you open the door of truth and step into that space with courage and a loving heart, new doors will continuously open as you are ready to step through them, furthering the exploration of the path.

My goal was to simply allow my process to gradually flow. Slowly, over time, I shared my story with people whom I trusted would accept it graciously and who would hold the space for me to tell it. I was becoming more comfortable in my new reality and felt ready to share my true story with my closest friends. There were many times in the past I wanted to share my true story with Michele, but I was not ready until now.

We had a lengthy conversation. I told her everything, and she listened and spoke with care and compassion. We talked in depth about the ending of the band, and I was able to explain my actions better, and in the context of my history, it made sense of what occurred on many levels. Some quirks of my personality were clear to her now. We laughed about realizing where my disturbing death-metal horror-scream singing style came from. We discussed how the band, our friendship, and everything surrounding it saved me.

I also confided in Cissy and later May and Annalyn. They were my oldest friends. We all attended St. Paul's together, and I wondered if they or anyone else they knew experienced anything similar. Having a conversation about an unspeakably tragic matter is incredibly difficult.

Almost one year later, Annalyn put me in touch with another victim of abuse from St. Paul's. It was the first time I connected with another person who had a shared experience.

Supportive relationships are where resilience comes from.

After two years of developing my personal Reiki practice, I was beginning to clearly recognize the beneficial results of using energy medicine as a healing tool. It was what gave me the courage, strength, and confidence to redirect the path I was on. It brought me to Vermont. I felt different and physically lighter; the subsequent effects of healing were becoming sharp and well-defined. I was still myself but an improved version. Besides the work with energy healing, truth served my authenticity. It was impossible to be truly genuine if I hid behind lies.

I opened my consciousness and the path of my heart in an emotionally connected way, identifying with what each of us are—a soul with a purpose. I worked to recognize how the ego functions to hide this fact. I experienced serendipitous moments and felt energy in a more structured way. Leaving behind my busy life gave me time to breathe, think, and just *be* for the first time.

Per Jean's recommendation, I spent time watching Oprah Winfrey's *Super Soul Sunday* and was inspired to read several books that would put me on the path of further understanding. The first was *The Seat of the Soul* by Gary Zukav, and the second was *A New Earth* by Eckhart Tolle. These books should be required reading for all humans. Using their tools and insight to have more of an understanding of how to interpret the situations I found myself in as a young person, I learned to establish more focused and reasonable thought patterns. They helped me to comprehend how anger and outrage, although fully justified, were just as damaging as the initial wounding. I was greatly inspired, and they led me down a rabbit hole of countless teachers and authors who helped shape my deeper awareness of healing from trauma.

During my first summer in Vermont, I completed Reiki Level III (Shinpiden) and received the master level attunement. In the early hours of the morning the first class was being held, I awoke to a surprising burst of strong energy pulsating through my entire body. I was familiar with how the energy felt as it flowed, and this was the strongest I had felt up to this point. I immediately looked at the time on the clock: 4:44 a.m.

I paid closer attention to numbers after my initial Reiki session with Jean. Now I recognized that number patterns were a method of communication from our guides and angels. I recorded and researched the patterns I was receiving.

In conversation with a fellow student in the master-level Reiki class, she mentioned she had been seeing a local medium who was gifted and had helped her a great deal.

I'd had a session with a medium once over twenty years earlier. It was an amazing experience, and I still hold close to some of the things she said. I made an appointment to see the medium immediately.

Since moving to Vermont, I had little contact with Mother. It was an important part of the initial stages of my healing journey to have separation. I was surprised at what a relief it was. Being disconnected from her was a positive experience for me. But after a few months, I received calls from a worried relative and a concerned neighbor of Mother, who informed me she was in the beginning stages of forgetfulness and erratic behavior. She was soon diagnosed with the initial stages of dementia. She knew the basics—her name, address, phone number, family members, and similar information—but was having difficulty managing money, purchasing food, and performing any other activity requiring a level of planning and coordination.

The calls became more frequent and urgent and the innate empathy that ruled my heart, often at my own expense, pulled me toward the thought of helping her in a moment of crisis. This concern and my experience of profound awakening made me believe a compassionate approach was necessary. I was nervous about stepping in to help, but I was her only option. My lifelong hope for a normal relationship with her came back into focus. Her health was deteriorating, and perhaps this would be the last chance to try. If things went well, we could have an honest and truthful conversation about what had happened.

I drove to Staten Island to get her on a Saturday, packed my car with her clothing and personal items, and settled in for the long drive home. She seemed different, happy to see me and grateful I had arrived to help her in an obvious time of distress. It was a long car ride back home, and she was as pleasant as she could have been, repeating how she was so appreciative of the offering of assistance and bringing her to live with me and my family. She tried to make conversation about random topics she thought I had an interest in, but it was short-lived. The art of conversation was a skill she did not possess. I thought to mention some of my unfortunate early happenings to see if this created an opportunity to talk about them, but I could not muster the courage. She slept for most of the ride.

After arriving back home, only a few hours went by before things completely soured. By evening, she became angry, combative, and rude—what I later learned was called "sundowning" in dementia patients. It was like she had gone backward thirty years and reverted to treating me like she did when I was a child. She mentioned old neighbors' names and other things from long ago. I immediately regretted my choice to bring her to my home.

The next morning, she was back to the behavior she showed when I first arrived at her apartment, appreciative and kind. As the day went on, she slipped backward again, and it became quickly apparent she needed a higher level of care than I could provide. She thought I was a young girl again. She asked me to get her cigarettes from the store and to clean the house. She was confused about who my children were and said inappropriate things in front of them, like how she wished she were dead. Noticing a few statues of Buddha, she told my children in an angry tone that they were Catholic and we should get rid of those things. They were frightened of her, and it sent me into a tailspin. The fear I saw in their eyes was the same fear I held in mine as a child. My ultimate focus as a parent was protecting my children and giving them a life better than what I had, and here I was compromising their well-being, and my own, by having her with us.

I called a local hotline for eldercare emergencies, and they recommended I bring her to the hospital for evaluation. It was winter in Vermont, and if she wandered out of the house in the middle of the night, things would end badly. I followed their advice, and, after some psychiatric testing, she was admitted. They contacted a long-term-care facility, to which she soon moved. I took care of all the arrangements and completed all the paperwork. Once she was settled, I had monthly check-ins by phone or text with the director of the facility. Her time with us had been less than forty-eight hours, and I regretted every second.

After I finished berating myself for putting my family in a difficult position and performing damage control, I had to get back to my personal work. As usual, I was a dependable helper. Mother was in a safe place where she was getting the level of care she needed, but my involvement going forward had to be from a distance. It was in my best interest to step away from her.

The relief of being in a new state hundreds of miles away from Mother was now compromised. She was not under my roof, but she was close. As usual, I was her designated next of kin and, due to the dementia diagnosis, her health care surrogate. I settled into the thought that the compassionate approach I took in helping her was the right one. My goal was to work on mending the feeling of losing my freedom from our toxic relationship and to find sovereignty over it instead.

The subject of after-death communication may cause discomfort to some readers but be inviting and welcoming to others. I have naturally leaned toward esoteric subjects throughout my life. I believe there is more available to us as humans than what we can perceive through the five senses. Like in Reiki or other forms of energy work where the practitioner serves as a conduit for universal energy, mediums serve in the same capacity to deliver messages from spirit. I believe we are spiritual-energy beings navigating human lives wherein we are supposed to learn prear-ranged lessons. Our consciousness lives after our body dies, and we continue the process of our soul's evolution. Spirit guides us toward our highest good and loves us unconditionally. Through mediumship, we can experience breathtaking moments of con-nection that can enhance and enrich our lives, making them joyful and brilliantly more beautiful. For many, it is easier to brush off connecting to the spirit world as farcical than it is to acknowledge the absolute greatness of it all.

As the last days of summer approached and the readiness to retreat within during the cold Vermont winter came upon us, I met with Celine, the recommended medium. As I was getting back on track with my journey after the bumps in the road, I hoped Celine could assist by providing deeper insight through messages my ancestors might have for me.

Celine welcomed me, sat, and closed her eyes. After a brief period of silent meditation, she spoke. "You are experiencing an awakening. You are like a college student experiencing new things, meeting new people, and going to new places. You are experiencing a higher frequency. It wasn't you. It was them."

The phrase "'It wasn't you, it was them" struck me. I did not ask her to elaborate, but my senses were heightened.

She was quiet for a moment, then continued, "On your left side is a grandmother figure, an *R* name. She is worried about you. She has her hand on your left shoulder. On your right side is your spirit guide, ancient, from the cosmos, a traveler, a star being. He has his hand on your right shoulder. He is always with you." A moment of quiet, then, "They want you to know you are on the right path."

I explained my connection to Reiki and the situation I had in the early morning of the master class a month prior, waking at 4:44 a.m. and receiving intense energy bursts through my whole body for several minutes. I told her of my experiences connecting to energy work over the last two years, including the spontaneous shamanic experience I had the previous year and how I was frightened by it.

Celine responded, "That was your attunement; you didn't need to go to the class. No one needs to have an intermediary between themselves and the spirit world." She explained, "Spirit backed off and will continue to reach you slowly and gently so as not to scare you."

I mentioned my interest in esoteric subjects and studies over the last twenty years and how I'd never had experiences like this before.

She responded, "This was important; it helped open your mind, but you were thinking about it intellectually, which was why you didn't experience awakening. You were also bogged down by fear and untruths. Now, your thinking is on a higher frequency level. Feeling. Being. Truthful. You have gifts. You are just like me. You must honor your true self. This is validation."

That night I dreamed I stood at the doorway of a black room. It was dark with no windows. The room felt heavy and sad. The walls turned into a bright sky-blue color, windows with billowing white curtains appeared, and the room became filled with sunshine and a warm, fresh breeze. The room felt light and happy, a place I wanted to be. I entered and smiled.

I had done considerable research about Vermont before moving, and the Reiki community there was part of it. I discovered the Vermont Reiki Association (VRA), which was founded in 2003 by a small group of practitioners and teachers. Over time, it grew from a small group to a much larger one and hosted a yearly conference and gathering of gifted speakers, teachers, and practitioners in the field of Reiki.

I joined the VRA as a member and attended their yearly fall conference, hoping to find a community to learn from and continue my personal work. I had been more comfortable with taking leaps. I applied and was accepted for an open board position. I wrote the quarterly newsletter, honing my writing skills while learning more about the organization. I was encouraged and inspired by the many members who worked to improve the lives of people in their communities through this healing work. I knew this was another crucial step on my journey.

Through my work with the VRA, I met Jennie, a seasoned and talented expressive-arts therapist. I was ready to add another therapeutic approach to my healing journey, and working with Jennie felt like the right start. Expressive-arts therapy adds to traditional talk therapy by exploring trauma and life's challenges through creative arts, such as painting, dancing, acting, drumming, singing, and writing. When I studied Reiki with Jean, she encouraged me to keep a journal, but at the time I found it difficult and wrote irregularly. I found it was just as hard to write down the inexpressible words that described my experiences as it was to verbalize them. By the time I started working with Jennie, I had made enough progress for the words to come easier, and when she encouraged me to write, I was ready. Writing proved to be an amazing source of healing. Once I started, I did not stop.

Working with Jennie helped me to connect to the areas of my unconscious mind that were blocked and stuck in the shock of trauma, shame, and fear. We slowly worked on bridging this gap by allowing my conscious mind to interpret my remembrances through focused arts. In a subtle and creative flow, this work brought an awareness of what could not be explained through speech. Over time, this approach helped to increase my ability to speak the words I had kept silent. It also allowed me to explore my relationship with a lost childhood. Accepting the reality of it and allowing myself to grieve this loss was the way to step out of the disregard I assigned to it. The time spent under Jennie's compassionate work and friendship was the passageway to gaining the ability and power to speak previously unspeakable words with a sense of authority over them. This work helped me to find my voice—my real, true, and unearthed voice.

After serving on the VRA board for one year, I was led to the next stage of my expedition. Being part of this community served me well, and I learned many lessons. My soul's personal work was underway, and I knew I had much more to uncover, although at the time I did not have a clear picture of what. Besides being more comfortable taking leaps of chance, I was now also becoming more comfortable with trusting my intentions, my intuition, and the guidance I was receiving. It was time to move forward.

Two months later, with great anticipation, I met Celine again. I was back in the flow of my healing work.

"Your spirit guide is ancient; he carries a bird on his arm and mentions the element of water. He is nature, a healer. Truth. He tells you information, but you do not always agree. It has been a long and winding road," Celine began. After a long moment of quiet, she continued, "A female figure is coming through. She has blonde hair. An *R* name again, but different from last time.

I thought of my aunt who passed the year before, but I did not remember her having blonde hair.

"It was blonde when you were young; you just don't remember. She liked how she looked with blonde hair. She mentions this in a feisty tone."

Yes, that was her.

She continued, "She says her passing was easy and comfortable. She knew everything; your mother confided in her. She was there when you cried into your pillow. She left you something special. It was quietly dealt with. They were told not to harm a man's reputation, especially a holy man. She took you to Disney to help you forget. You are not the only one. It was boys and girls."

I felt a lump in my throat. My aunt had come through to speak the truth. After all these years, the truth, delivered with such accuracy, was wholly unmistakable. The pillow, the jewelry box, the trip, and those sickening words that never left me since the day they were uttered.

"They are standing together, both bowing toward you with their hands clasped in prayer. They are saying you are sacred, an earth angel. Your work must continue. It is vital. They are proud of who you have become in the face of deep adversity. You have new breath. You must care for yourself and set healthy boundaries. Do not back down. You must feel safe. It is now time for those who were abused. It is okay to care of yourself. Your mother was abused too; she never took care of herself."

I always wondered if something had happened to Mother to cause the emotional void in her heart, but my own trauma kept me trapped in my own personal and isolated misery of shame.

Celine closed her eyes and breathed deeply, then spoke. "Who is this coming through? It is a female energy. She says she was told it was to help the children who were in vulnerable situations. She thought they were offering help and counseling. She did not know at first. She picked the children with disabilities and those from broken homes to set up meetings with the fathers. She is terribly sorry that once she found out what was happening, she did not do anything to stop it. She continued to provide help in selecting the children. There was no turning back. How could she resolve that type of sin? There were many over the decades. She took those secrets to her grave."

Celine asked, "Is this making sense to you?"

Every word she spoke was a startling account of what occurred and contained answers I had been searching for over many decades. It was Sister Mary Darcy. Like my aunt, she came through to speak her truth. I was wide-eyed, mouth ajar.

"I can see him. The Priest. He is showing himself. He will not speak. He is holding a large cross he wears around his neck, like a tool for hypnotizing, dangling and swaying it back and forth. He put children in a dark room to scare them and come to their rescue."

A large and important part of my investigation into my past and my healing work was deconstructing this intense moment of trauma. The Priest did leave me in a dark room in the rectory before the abuse happened. The validating details Celine provided were disturbing to hear. I clearly remembered the large cross he wore. I was thoroughly shaken by this conversation. Our first session was general, but this one was explosive. I had received my greatest longing—validation.

On the ride home, I recalled an interaction with my aunt during a barbeque at her home several years prior. I had stepped into the house to get some napkins, and she was at the sink, washing dishes with her back to me. I said hello and we chatted about my children, the weather, and normal things. Her voice became shaky and cracked. She shut the water off, dried her hands, and faced me. Tears streamed down her face.

"Don't let anyone ever hurt you! Do you hear me, Kathleen? Do not let anyone ever hurt you. You don't deserve that!"

Someone entered the kitchen, and she went back to washing the dishes. I put my hand on her shoulder and said, "Don't worry, I'm fine." The enduring lie of my life. Looking back now, I wish I had the capacity to continue the conversation. After thirty years of keeping the secret, she could no longer bear it, yet we lost the opportunity to share the truth that day in the kitchen. Afterward, I slipped right back into comfortable muteness and never approached the subject with her again, until the day when the conversation was continued through Celine. She finally spoke her truth, and I was deeply appreciative of it.

This was the first time that information about Mother's experience with abuse was spoken about, and it opened my eyes to the larger picture I could not see before.

Abuse confuses the victim into thinking they are completely alone. That they are the only ones traumatized and hurt so deeply that no one else could empathize or even believe it is true. This is part of what keeps us silent.

The serendipitous moments continued. Unexpectedly, soon after this session, my cousin sent me a photograph of her mother, my aunt, herself, and two other cousins when they were children, standing on a balcony overlooking a large lake. My aunt had a big blonde 1960s' bouffant.

I had always held an interest in the topic of death and after-death communication, but these sessions with Celine sparked my wonder. I revisited the subject by rereading *Journey of Souls*, by Michael Newton, and *Life After Life*, by Raymond Moody Jr. I followed up with several other books and listened to podcasts. I read *Many Lives, Many Masters* by Brian Weiss, which delves into the subject of past lives, reincarnation, and soul evolution.

In the Western world, these topics have gained some ground but are still largely misunderstood. Understanding our soul's journey and the lessons we are here to learn gives a greater sense of purpose to life and a deeper perception of the challenges we face.

The work I had been doing since arriving in Vermont and the sessions with Celine helped to deconstruct and bring clarity to my memory.

But regaining traumatic memories is unsettling. Often, traumatic remembrances are not a complete story; they are held in fragments. There is often no neat beginning, middle, or end to them; they are hard to convey and tell in sequence, due to the loss of executive functioning. The intense difficulty in processing and speaking about trauma causes stress hormones to spike and delivers the effect of reexperiencing the trauma. Whether held in secret or not, trauma interferes with all aspects of life; it does not matter how many years have passed.

Throughout my life, I had maintained control by dissociating from and suppressing inner chaos. Since the chaos had been let loose, I felt like I was upside down yet also more clearheaded. Even so, the thought that no one would believe me thrived, as it always had, and I was aware how coming out and telling my story would make me susceptible to hurtful and insensitive comments.

Each step I took flowed to the next in small and big ways. I again received photos from my cousin. They were from the Disney vacation, taken after my rape in the rectory. I never saw any photos from this trip before. I stared at them for lengthy periods of time. The pictures were a little blurry, but much stood out to me. I could see a forced smile on my face. My face showed a sadness, my head was down, and my body was crumpled in a bent-forward position. It looked as if I carried an invisible heavy bag on my back and had a leash around my neck, being pulled along through what was supposed to be the happiest place on earth.

This gift provided an opportunity to tell my cousin the truth. My efforts to get answers were falling into place in a timely way, and I found the courage to seize the moment. She admitted she was struck by my strange behavior during the vacation, where I was quiet, distant, and not having fun. I did not want any souvenirs and didn't want to eat or go on rides. Her words gave me further validation.

As I sat across from Celine three months after our explosive second session, I explained to her how recently I had been feeling more connected to spirit, seeing things out of the corner of my eye—flashes of light and number patterns. I heard my name spoken clearly in the middle of the night again.

"The archangels are with you. They are saying, 'Keep steady. This is validation. Yes, you are hearing and seeing; this is the beginning, and energetic adjustments are being made.' They are learning how to best work with you. They are smiling. Also, you will have answers from Ancestry. Someone else will come forward with their story of abuse, and you will support each other. Your aunt is with you and will remain throughout the process."

I had not mentioned to Celine my intentions to do research on Ancestry. I had completed the DNA test but had not yet gone any further. When I arrived home, I revisited my results and focused on the section that provides DNA matches to other users. I saw I was paired with two young men who showed elevated levels of matched strands and were categorized as first cousins. I did not recognize their names, and their locations did not make any sense. A connection of some sort was obvious, but I was not ready to reach out, still learning how to be in the flow of the information I received. It had to move at its own speed. It could not be rushed or hurried.

In time, I would know everything.

Chapter Ten

THE ARC OF
THE MORAL UNIVERSE

In October 1992, Sinéad O'Connor was the musical guest on *Saturday Night Live*. She sang an a cappella version of Bob Marley's song "War," which she amended to protest child sexual abuse in the Roman Catholic Church. She changed the lyric from "racism" to "child abuse." She held a photo of Pope John Paul II to the camera while singing the word "evil" and tore the photo into pieces while saying, "Fight the real enemy." She threw the ripped pieces toward the camera. Outrage ensued, not toward the church but toward her. Angry demonstrators gathered outside her performances. She courageously spoke up for survivors everywhere. She was brave enough to speak the truth on live television, yet she was chastised and condemned for doing so. She was my hero. Even so, I was not yet ready to find my voice and would remain silent about what happened to me for another twenty-three years.

The following week the actor who hosted the show held the tape-repaired photo of the pope and announced how he would have "given her such a smack" if he were there, garnering loud applause and laughter from the studio audience. Threatening violence toward a woman who spoke up about the sexual abuse of children by clergy was applauded and laughed at. The scenario was used as fodder for further humiliating her. This sent a clear message to victims of abuse: coming forward with allegations and speaking your truth against the most powerful religious institution in the world, the Catholic Church, will only subject you to further shame, rebuke, and intimidation.

Historically, the church's power and substantial influence allowed it to escape responsibility for its part in countless cases of abuse and cover-ups. At the time, this power still reigned strong; however, it soon faltered for the first time in history.

Injustice seems to move like lightning, while true and deserved justice seems to move slowly.

During this same year, author Jason Berry released a book, *Lead Us Not into Temptation*, a story of the cover-up of sexual abuse within the Catholic Church. The book was a chronicle of the hierarchy of church leaders who had covered up the abuse of hundreds of children in what he described as the "Watergate" of the church. But no one listened.

At the time, the Catholic Church in the United States had quietly funded over four hundred million dollars to settle hundreds of cases of clergy abuse. In every case, there were rules allowing for documents to be sealed and nondisclosure agreements to be signed. A decade after Sinéad's protest performance on live television, the cover-up of child sexual abuse within the church was finally acknowledged by John Paul II, who admitted his gross negligence and irreverent failings to protect children during his twenty-seven-year reign. He finally acknowledged the church's role in the concealment of the abuse of countless numbers of innocent children. One year later, the Vatican announced it would use papal courts to try priests suspected of abuse. The trials were kept secret and only served to emphasize their attempts to hide their crimes and to protect the perpetrators.

Cardinal Joseph Ratzinger was given the job of dispensing

specific guidelines on how to deal with what became known as "the problem." To dioceses worldwide, he attached to his guidelines a cover sheet specifically asking recipients not to disclose the information contained therein.

In 2006, as settlement numbers reached $2.6 billion, Ratzinger became pope and the abuse crisis reached all corners of the globe. His own extensive history of covering up abuse was also revealed, as was that of his brother.

Doctrinal Christianity is the major adversary of free thought. From their pulpits and with blind adherence from their pews, church leaders have enabled the suppression of those who did not agree with their brand of dogma for centuries, in both subtle and forceful ways.

The church suppressed and demonized all other spiritual practices, the divine feminine, science, and enlightenment. They created the greatest story ever told, molded in the pursuit of power and greed, and whose lessons were manipulated by political leaders and used as a form of control. They rewrote history, assumed ownership of pagan celebrations and rituals, dictated unyielding arbitrary rules, and removed by force anyone who dared challenge them.

Superstitions and the rebuke of science still exist in many forms and cause many of the overarching problems pervading society today.

The existence of spiritual phenomena and divine miracles recorded since the earliest days of humanity threatened the church's cautiously constructed dogma. The worship of nature, mother earth, and feminine leadership were their enemies. The church attributed the intricacies of earth-based spiritual practices to the actions of evil and sorcery as they proceeded to nurture war, conflict, and rivalry around the globe in the quest for power. Humanity continues to suffer the consequences of the loss of the sacred feminine, spiritual healing practices, and the reverence of nature.

The repercussions of these losses bring us to the extreme challenges we are facing today. Throughout history, many of the church's actions are the definition of double standards. Its leaders, priests, and clergy have secured themselves positions of hierarchy, yet the personal actions of many are directly opposite of the moral code dispensed by their institutions. The abuse of children under their care has been a quiet issue since its early stages, and the elevation and protection of abusers are a constant companion to these grotesque acts. The parishioners, patrons, and followers of the church must demand fundamental structural changes for anything to truly change, although it seems unlikely. How does one connect to the divine with one's head buried in the sand?

The papacy and government of the Roman Catholic Church are elaborately structured and are the oldest absolute monarchy in the world. It is a system based on self-preservation and not subject to standard checks and balances by any outside electoral, judicial, or legislative body. This position acutely upholds its culture of patriarchy, narcissism, hypocrisy, and unimpeded abuses and has flourished for centuries under their code of silence. It is this cult of secrecy that has unabashedly protected their power. A turn-a-blind-eye culture permeates their ranks. They have been willing to let a few suffer to preserve their dominance.

Humanity was blindfolded for centuries but is gradually waking up to what cannot be hidden any longer. The voices of truth are being heard. For the good of us all, we must adhere to a sincere effort to preserve the basic dignity and common good of all human persons. We must see how religious fervor and limiting ideologies only serve to muddy the waters.

In 2002, the *Boston Globe* published its report on investigations into sexual abuse in the Catholic Church, finally breaking the seal of silence. The ensuing movie version, *Spotlight*, won an Oscar and brought about just public outrage. According to a study by the John Jay College of Criminal Justice, from 1950 to 2002, a total of 4,392 priests were accused of abuse. I suspect this number would have doubled if all victims found the courage to come forward.

As public knowledge grew, church leaders scrambled and looked for new ways to protect themselves and their assets. They would find one through bankruptcy, a structured process for settling large numbers of lawsuits while preserving as many assets as possible. Dioceses restructured holdings to shrink the value of their estates before the process of bankruptcy filings and reaching settlements, which would have a percentage of the dioceses' assets allocated to victims. A simple inquiry into the closing of many Catholic schools and the shrinking of dioceses would reveal most closings were the results of lawsuit settlements and related efforts to preserve their wealth. An additional benefit to this process was the possibility of secrecy.

Lawsuits and trials lead to publicity, while bankruptcy provides a quieter end to claims of abuse and is structured to prevent additional litigation. Today, the wealth of the church is estimated to be in the trillions, with large investments in real estate, banking, insurance, and other areas of finance. Between their holdings, their charities, their exemption from all taxes, and their vast amount of priceless art, the church is one of the wealthiest institutions on the planet. The actual amount is almost impossible to calculate due to its sheer vastness as well as the lack of accounting oversight into the finances run by their own banks. Yet small and large parishes cloak themselves in robes of poverty, taking the hard-earned money of their parishioners and offering pittances to survivors of abuse, whose lives were forever altered by their abusers and the church's failed leadership.

The church would also create a program called the Independent Reconciliation and Compensation Program (IRCP).

Starting in New York in 2016, it spread to other states to mediate the mounting cases. This program processed claims of sexual abuse by clergy by offering compensation outside of legal channels, with the caveat that claimants, upon agreement to receive compensation, would give up their right to further legal action. Many claimants filed through an online form without the advice or representation of a lawyer.

Later reporting from the *New York Daily News* in January 2021 revealed a conference call transcript received from a 2017 meeting between the lawyer and administrator of the program, Kenneth Feinberg, and representatives of three Upstate New York dioceses. The IRCP program was only created to thwart the passing of the Child Victims Act. Mr. Feinberg stated the cardinal (Dolan) was worried the legislature was coming close to passing the statute, and they were taking care of their own problem.

"We want to be able to show Albany that people are accepting this money and signing releases. You don't need to change the statute."

The long arm of the law further reached into the fight against child sexual abuse by clergy in September 2018, when Barbara Underwood, the New York State attorney general, launched an investigation into the Roman Catholic Church to inspect and examine the cover-up of the alleged widespread abuses of minors. The statewide action was the first of its kind. All eight dioceses in the state received subpoenas as part of a civil investigation.

On the heels of a recently released and scathing Pennsylvania investigative report, Ms. Underwood stated, "Victims in New York deserve to be heard as well—and we are going to do everything in our power to bring them the justice they deserve."[9] The church responded by saying they were ready and eager to work with her in the investigation.

Ms. Underwood also advocated for the New York State Legislature to pass the languishing Child Victims Act bill, which would allow all victims to file civil suits until age fifty and seek criminal charges until age twenty-eight. From 2011 to 2018, eight states, including New York, were close to passing similar legislation.

The church spent $10.6 million lobbying against the bills at the same time they said repeatedly how they wanted to be held accountable and make amends to victims.

Ms. Underwood urged any victim of sexual abuse by Catholic clergy, or anyone with knowledge of abuse, to come forward and participate in the probe. A telephone and web report hotline were established for members of the public to volunteer their stories.

I made the decision to come forward and tell my story. For the first time, it was told to legal authorities. I followed up by filing a claim through the IRCP. After first speaking the truth about this tragic part of my life in 2016, just two years later I was fortunate enough to have the opportunity to speak my truth in this format. It provided the stark realization that I did not stand alone but with the countless other survivors who were able to find their voices. This cult of abusers and their enablers required the full weight of justice to defeat them, not a shut-up money-compensation program.

Signed into law by New York governor Andrew Cuomo on Valentine's Day 2019, the Child Victims Act[10] was an arduous fight and a victory for victims who had long lobbied to seek justice from abusers and their enablers. The three main components of the act were to extend the statute of limitations to allow for criminal charges against sexual abusers of children until their victims turned twenty-eight for felony cases, up from the current twenty-three; to allow victims to seek civil action against their abusers and institutions who enabled them until they turned fifty-five; and to open a one-year, one-time-only period to allow all victims to seek civil action regardless of how long ago the abuse occurred.

The bill had languished for years at the state capitol due to strong resistance by the Republican majority and fierce opposition from the Catholic Church. Their insurance representatives, through lobbyists, worked with the Republican-controlled state senate to repeatedly block the measure to repeal the antiquated and predator-friendly statute of limitations, even as it was passed in the Democratic-led assembly.

Democrats won control in November 2018, and the whole dynamic changed. Once the church knew the act was likely to pass, they dropped their opposition after language was added for public institutions to be similarly sued during the one-year period. The look-back period opened six months later, on August 14, 2019.

After the Child Victims Act was signed into law, I, along with thousands of other survivors in New York City, made the choice to further seek justice by retaining legal counsel. Justice for victims in the form of legal action against abusers and the institutions who protected them regardless of how long ago these crimes occurred was now possible. The IRCP settlement offer was officially refused and, through my counsel, I was able to formally bring charges, over three decades later, against my abusers, who were now known as defendants in New York Supreme Civil Court. The Perpetrators were now held accountable for their heinous actions.

Although the arc is bending toward justice now, I will continue to live with the consequences of their cruelty for the rest of my life. This is part of my story forever.

Decades later, what does justice feel like for survivors like me who never thought this day would come? There is a simple answer: Relief. The weight of the burden is taken from the survivors and put on the backs of the criminals who rightly deserve to carry it.

Sex-abuse scandals exist in nearly every patriarchal organized religious institution—the Catholic Church, the Southern

Baptists, the United Methodist Church, Protestant churches, Jehovah's Witnesses, the Boy Scouts, and countless other religious and youth-centered groups who use trust, faith, and authority to repugnantly carry out, enable, and conceal the sexual abuse of innocent children and adults. It is not only in religious institutions where these abuses flourish but also in sports and athletic programs, in the entertainment industry, and in many other areas of living where a person can hold power over another.

As I pieced together the puzzle of my life, I found my overall experience attending Catholic school would have completely stripped away any feelings of connection to the Catholic faith, even if the traumatic sexual abuse did not happen. The behaviors of the nuns and priests, ranging from physical and mental abuse to judgmental and mean attitudes to criminal and grotesque acts, left me not only feeling disconnected but filled with abhorrence and in a state of constant emotional distress. Researching the institutional historical data of the church helped me to grasp its history and further developed my search for and awareness of truth.

The truth is the truth, and no one can hide from it.

In June 2020, the Archdiocese of New York announced the closure of twenty Catholic schools, blaming the COVID–19 pandemic. Over the years, many Catholic schools have merged or closed due to low enrollment.

St. Paul's Catholic School closed in 2008. In 2011, a merger reopened the school as St. Peter St. Paul School. In 2020, the school was on the list of closures. Good riddance.

During the time I conducted this research, I had a vivid dream. I was in a room in a large Victorian mansion. The room resembled a library, with shelves and stacks of books. I wore a red sleeveless tank top and searched for something hidden in one of the books. Suddenly, a strong wind picked up and a demonic creature appeared before me. It was Sister Mary Darcy, appearing as a skeletal figure dressed in flowing black robes and a nun habit. She snarled at me, exposing her teeth, and reached in my direction. Her eyes were empty black holes. I took deep breaths, each deeper than the one before it, filling my body with intense energy. I stood in front of her without a hint of fear and directed the force of concentrated energy toward her. It threw her backward. She disappeared and the wind stopped.

My healing work, investigation, and the writing of this book have stirred the spirits on the other side who were involved.

Some want the truth to be told, some are evolving because of it, and some, the unevolved spirits, are angry. Although docile in her first appearance during my session with Celine, this time I believe Sister Mary Darcy visited me in the dream to frighten me into silence like she did when I was a child. I fought back and banished her, retrieving the soul part she had stolen from me long ago. My light is a thousand times stronger than her darkness. It always was.

The process of excavating the past to free me from it was working, but the deeper I dug, the more information was revealed, and the somber puzzle of what happened began to take shape one piece at a time.

Chapter Eleven

INTOLERABLE TRUTHS

As my research unfolded, my memories gained clarity, and I continued to receive validations. My demand for truth was strong, and when it was met by the vulgarly shocking confession from Mother as she neared the end of her life, I was overwhelmed with grief.

After learning of Mother's admission of sexual abuse, I felt as if I had been knocked down a flight of a thousand stairs. I landed at the bottom, battered and bruised. It took time to accept and mourn this information. It was an intense struggle to process those words. No wonder I was such a mess growing up. This revelation changed things. This was the long-suffering secret that produced the anonymous unease I had felt throughout my life, and, sadly, I was confident it was not the only one. As much as I knew about what happened to me, this proved there was more I was not aware of. I intuitively knew Mother's confession was just the beginning. Learning this sad fact caused a great deal of pain, but it also did the opposite. It provided validation and an intense demand for the whole truth. If I could find it, I would be set free. In the end, I was right. The truth will set you free. It is not just a cliché or a catchphrase. There has never been a more sincere statement.

The healing work I had been engrossed in proved to be a useful medicine. It gave me the power to counter deeply unbearable wounds. Without it, I do not know where the news could have taken me. I had learned to allow myself to feel the grief it brought but at the same time hold sovereignty over it. It was a master class in learning how to tolerate the intolerable.

Survivors of sexual abuse hold a range of emotions but often are likely to feel the abuse is somehow their fault.

Her confession allowed me to realize I'd been set up for failure from the start. The notion I held about how she may have been part of the planning with the nun and priests, not just the cover-up, also felt more tangible now. Although this information answered fundamental questions and released me from its veiled concealment, it also broke me in an intense way and left me with many new questions, taking my ongoing investigation to a new level.

After the confession, I struggled with my decision and the actions I took in finding the compassion to bring Mother to Vermont. I had once again been taken advantage of by a narcissistic sociopath and put my best interest away to deal with her. Everything was up to me, like it had always been.

Prior to helping her, I had not spoken to her in over a year. I wanted her out of my life. I had uprooted myself and my family and moved from New York to Vermont to leave a painful past behind and start a new life. Yet, there I was, just six months later, upending everything to provide care for her. I regretted my decision and wished I had left her to stew in misery, just as she had done to me as a child. I was steeped in familiar rage.

In the weeks following, I reviewed the text conversation with Roseanne so many times I could recite it verbatim. As painful as it was to hear, this truth was what I needed to fully comprehend our strange history. It liberated me just as much as it completely crushed me.

When terrible truths from your past are revealed, they stir your nervous system, and long-forgotten memories gradually resurface. As each is validated, more appear in a deliberately gentle way as you are ready to receive them. For me, memories usually appear in the early morning hours, just before fully waking, in the form of thoughts, dreams, words, and numbers. The first memory that surfaced soon after my conversation with Roseanne was of me as a small child standing in a vegetable garden surrounded by a twisted array of vines and scratchy leaves with small bright-red tomatoes hanging from the stems. The second memory was of me sleeping above the pillows at the top of the bed I shared with Mother as a child, a pull-out couch in the living room of our small apartment. I lay with the pillows at my back, trying to fall asleep. The mice lived in the gap between the bed frame and the back of the couch. These memories were wretchedly visceral. Forgetting was the only way to preserve myself.

At the same time, knowing this cruel truth has helped to solve the greatest mystery of my life and has given me the answer to the question I always asked myself: "Why doesn't Mother love me?" I now realized that when she looked at me, she remembered the hideous, unfathomable abuses she inflicted upon me at a tender age. I wondered why Mother had not ever shown me affection and realized she was never able to hug me, comfort me, or touch me in a normal motherly way. Her actions, which took place so early in my life, formed a wall between us. She held many secrets, but this was the most horrendous. She truly saved her worst for me.

After much soul searching and work to regulate myself, I understood that if I had not brought Mother to Vermont, I would have never known this shocking truth—and therefore never been freed from its secret clutches. But once my anger quelled and became malleable, softening into plain and pure sadness, I allowed myself to recognize how it was in my best interest to find compassion.

It always is. Finding compassion for others is also finding it for yourself.

As difficult as it was, hearing her admission of guilt was an important part of my healing journey. The weight of nameless trauma spread through me like a menacing cancerous growth, full of shame and fear. It was pervasive and elusive at the same time, alive inside of me, lurking in the shadows of my memory. Now, it was named. These sorrowful words were spoken from pits of darkness to meet my ears and to be held in the light of my healing work, to be cleansed, and to be released. I was unequivocally ready for this next stage of my journey and unquestionably sure I would soon learn more of my story.

It had been four months since my last session with Celine. I hoped this next session would bring more awareness about what happened during my early years and that spirit could provide useful information.

"They are waiting to guide her across," Celine began. "It could be soon; there is congestion forming in her chest. This is a female relative, elderly. If you are thinking about seeing her, you should do it soon. They are saying she stinks; she is mean and grouchy, and no one wants to care for her because of that. She just sits in a chair."

I understood she was referring to Mother. Anger rose in me.

"I am seeing a field. Continue to spend time in nature; it is important. There has been an influx of information that has come and will continue to come to you. You need to find balance. I see a white duck. It came to you as a spiritual messenger. I see you smiling, riding a bike. You are free from something that was holding you down. Congratulations. Your frequency is raised. I see you at the top of a ladder, looking down."

Celine continued, "I'm seeing the yellow flowers with brown in the middle. I do not know why they called them 'black-eyed' when they are clearly 'brown-eyed.' This is related to your sacral chakra and courage."

Mother shared a name with those flowers. As usual, although I did not mention it aloud, Celine followed my thoughts.

"She was abused. By a male relative. The abuse continued for a long time, even after she was married. She had babies, more than one that she gave away. She became an abuser herself because for the first time in her life it made her feel like she was the one in control. She knew it was wrong, but she did it anyway."

I had been stoic in the days leading to this session, keenly focused on facts and learning the truth, but after Celine spoke those words, I could not stop the tears. As I had hoped, spirit conveyed what I needed to know. Celine and I had a long conversation about the nature of healing, trauma, and how it was passed on from generation to generation. I was grateful to have her share her vast knowledge and deep kindness and care with me.

I reviewed my notes while sitting in the car after the session and thought about the white duck Celine mentioned. The prior weekend while at the lake I'd waded into the water to cool down. A large white duck landed close by. It sat floating in the water for an unusually long time, staring at me. It stayed so long I started talking to it. I asked if it was lost, or from a nearby farm. It was an odd encounter. This session provided more validation and vital details about Mother's abuse and about births before my siblings. This abuse fractured her life and eventually led her to become an abuser herself. Finding out who her abuser was would lead to more answers.

By this time, I was diligently researching Ancestry, forming a time line of names and relationships in coordination with other online resources, such as property records and other identifying materials. I was now in an intense pursuit of piecing together the puzzle of my life.

In early January, I was contacted through Ancestry's messaging service by one of the young men I matched with. I assumed it was a connection from Father's side of the family, which I knew little about. Through my research, I had found my paternal grandmother and her parents and siblings. I mentioned their last name in our correspondence, but it did not seem to add up. He informed me his mother, Victoria, had been adopted in New York in 1952 and knew her biological mother's last name. It matched my maternal family name. Born prematurely in the summer of 1952, and transferred to The New York Foundling, Victoria was adopted by a couple from Long Island. She was diagnosed with cerebral palsy, a disorder that impacted but never defined her life. She was raised in a loving home with caring parents. After college, she left New York and spent decades as an early special education teacher in a struggling school district in California, a mentor to many students.

After gaining the courage to ask a relative who I thought may have known, I was able to confirm the details firsthand. This relative was shocked by the information I had found and told me she was there when the baby was born. She helped Mother complete the adoption paperwork. She was the only one who knew besides the father. She cried and told me how she never forgot her name, Victoria, and that she thought of her each year on her birthday. I replied to Victoria's son with all the details. He passed it along to his mother, and we planned to meet for a video call the following day.

I had a sister! My mind raced. What would I say? Would we have a chance to meet in person? I felt excited and happy to have found her. It seemed she had a good life; she was the lucky one. Her life would not have been so good if Mother had kept her, I was sure of it. I went to sleep looking forward to the opportunity to meet her the next day via video call. Her name, Victoria, rolled off my tongue and through my brain; it felt familiar. As the name spun around in my thoughts, I remembered Victoria was the name Mother used to tell me she wanted to name me, but Father did not like it and chose Kathleen instead.

When I woke the next morning, I had a new message from Victoria's son. I excitedly opened the message, expecting to see a time for the meeting.

"I'm sorry to tell you this; Mom passed away last night. I feel like I'm in a movie with the coincidence of you giving her closure with this story. Before she went to sleep, I read her your email and told her she had a sister. She was happy to find this out. There were some physical illness setbacks she experienced over the last few years, but her passing was unexpected. She had a heart attack in her sleep."

I was completely disoriented by this whirlwind of news, which had ended on such a sad note—just as abruptly as it began. Victoria had lived courageously and fully, had a happy marriage and a beautiful son, and although we never had a chance to meet, I deeply mourned her passing.

One month later, I heard from the second young man listed in the Ancestry DNA matches. Like my newly found nephew, he also messaged me.

"It looks like we have a high result of matched DNA in common, along with my brother and sister. Somehow, we are related but I'm not exactly sure how. I always thought my father, brother, sister, and I looked a little different than the rest of the family, and I have always been curious to see if we had any other close family we didn't know about. Do you have any idea what the connection is?"

After trading a few messages, and over the course of three weeks and in similar fashion, a confession from a relative of his told the true story. It was confirmed how Mother had given birth to his father, my half brother, in early 1955 and had given him up for adoption. His adoptive parents never told him the truth about his birth, and learning the truth was shocking. We never spoke. In the end, I hoped he was able to find the peace only truth can provide.

In the span of two months, I acquired two half siblings, one of whom I found and lost in twenty-four hours and one I had no contact with.

There may be more.

This enabled me to fill in more pieces of the puzzle and to add additional names and dates to my research and investigation. Each time I felt ready to take the next step, doors continued to open and new information appeared, leading me further and further on this journey of discovery.

Nine months and a dizzying amount of new information later, my next meeting with Celine finally arrived. As the cold retreated and the warmer spring air surfaced, I reflected on the amount of resolute healing work I had undertaken over the winter. We spoke in depth about Reiki and other forms of energy medicine, including sound healing, which I wanted to explore.

"I see you smiling and steering a sailboat. You are alone. You have gathered all the information you needed from mentors, and now it is time for you to use it. I see a gift. They are saying, 'You are the gift.' Deep down you know that. I see gold. You have blossomed and have given birth to yourself. You have gifts to share. Take notes and write everything down. It may feel like you are talking to yourself, but the voice inside your head is your higher self. Keep the messages clear. You are at a fork in the road. Go in the direction that puts a smile on your face. Use the information you have gathered."

After many months of inner work, it was nice to hear these words.

"You are graduating. People will be looking for you, they will know you, and you will know them. They will sense your vibration, your frequency. I see you rolling dice, smiling. You oversee your own destiny; there is no right or wrong. Connect with your inner voice. It is like gathering a handful of berries. Some will be riper than others, some juicier. Feel into your connection. When you sense fear, ask, 'What do you want me to know?' You are a helper; you have come a long way. You have turned it around, and now you can give back. It was never your fault. You gave yourself a higher education."

She smiled. "Keep learning from the shaman you have been working with. It is okay to take a few steps back. It can be overwhelming at first, sometimes frightening."

I had not mentioned to Celine I was working with a shaman.

Chapter Twelve

RECLAIMING MY POWER

S hamanism is an ancient spiritual practice and ancestor to all formal religions, which, in their early stages, shared the shamanic thread of connection to the divine. The word "shaman," "the one who knows," comes from the Tungus tribe of Siberia and means "a person who possesses esoteric knowledge and the extraordinary adeptness to act as an intermediary between the human and spirit worlds." Shamans have been found universally in all the cultures of the world and date back tens of thousands of years. By entering an altered state of consciousness, they can inhabit a place unrestrained by time and space, assisted by helping spirits, allies, and power-animal guides. They move between a non-ordinary reality, or dreamtime world of spirit, and the physical world. Although much of the modern world dismisses this sacred work, shamanism, a form of energy medicine, has worked its way into the mainstream over the last fifty years as a complementary healing practice. Today's shamans are the bridge between this ancient tradition and the modern world, bringing a multifaceted approach to individual and community healing.[11]

Working with a shamanic healer is an effective and powerful way to relieve trauma. Trauma steals your personal power by creating dysfunction in the mental, emotional, and physical bodies. Shamanic treatment methods are based on the restoration of lost power and the awakening of true healing.

Soon after my introduction to and training in Reiki with Jean Bromage, I began learning about shamanism. Peculiar and mysterious happenings surfaced as I delved into this topic, including the spontaneous shamanic experience that sent me hiding under my blanket in the middle of the night. I was not ready then, but I knew I would explore the world of shamanism when the time was right.

I met Wendy Halley at the Mind Body Spirit conference in Burlington, Vermont, in the early spring of 2019. The conference, organized by Celine, featured an array of esoteric practitioners from Vermont and the surrounding area. I attended the conference as a volunteer for the Vermont Reiki Association. Wendy occupied the table next to ours.

When I approached to say hello, I knew I was stepping into the next phase of my journey. I asked about her practice, the beautiful handmade drums she crafted and had on display, her shamanic healing work, and the interesting Energy Genesis explained in a pamphlet at the front of the display. The Energy Genesis was a noninvasive healing chamber that used a specific combination of light and sound frequencies to create a resonance within its 360-degree interior, providing a deep state of rest. We chatted for a bit, and I mentioned my interest in shamanic healing work and soul retrieval. The following day, I contacted Wendy to arrange an appointment to get started.

My goal was to regain the power I lost through trauma, hoping it would address the unrelenting fear and endless feelings of being unsafe I had exhaustingly learned to live with. I hoped the ancestral-lineage component of the unresolved trauma passed down from generation to generation would also be tackled. This was a topic I had been learning about since my sessions with Celine, when I realized I was not the only one.

Between the time I met Wendy and our scheduled appointment date, I learned of Mother's confession. Wendy and her work entered my life at a significant moment and would become an essential and influential part of my healing.

Wendy, also a seasoned psychotherapist, began the session with a get-to-know-you conversation. As I was now more comfortable talking about my past, I explained my history, the personal work I had been doing, and the recent and shocking confession of Mother. It was the first time I had shared those words I had received ten days prior with another person. As much as I had confided in Alex, I had not been ready to share this with him, and I knew he was not ready to hear it.

It can be distressing to learn of or be witness to the suffering and pain experienced by another person, especially someone you love dearly. When exposed to disturbing details of traumatic events, one can experience what is known as secondary trauma. This type of trauma can also occur in emergency workers who serve in natural disasters or therapists and social workers who treat clients with PTSD. Children who are exposed to violence in their surroundings, even if not physically harmed personally, can still develop the same trauma responses as the victim. My history impacted him.

In time and with care, I did share the unfortunate news.

I knew I had been guided to Wendy well before I received the hideous news, to have this healing session in place as an additional safety net. My story was shocking and sad, and I needed all the support I could get. However, each time I revealed its hideous details, I was further relieved of its weight and thankful for the opportunity to do so. Talking was therapeutic, but when combined with deep healing work for the soul, it was life-changing.

We moved on to the healing session after a supportive conversation. Wendy explained how she begins with a brief opening ceremony before entering an altered state of consciousness supported by a monotonous drumbeat. Once in the altered state, she connects with her helper spirits and invites them to attend to the issues we discussed. When the healing is complete, she provides a narration of what occurred. As I lay on the table, my ears felt pressure, as if I were climbing at a high altitude. I felt a presence behind me and on the sides of my upper body. I relaxed and settled in.

Soon the smell of smoke from burning sage filled the room while I lay comfortably on the table. It surrounded me with soothing, fragrant wisps. Rain fell hard outside and was the perfect accompaniment to the shamanic drumbeat entering and blending with an added rattle, loud and pulsating. My body was quickly filled with the familiar flow of energy. Wendy lyrically let out a calling whistle, which invited her guides' presence to assist in the dreamtime. It filled the room and landed on top of the rain, drums, and rattle in perfect unison.

Entering the lower world, Wendy and her guide came upon a dark landscape with arched shadows, which formed the towering outline of a city. It was night. In the center stood an abandoned hotel. It was an art deco–influenced design, clearly once grand but now a decaying and dilapidated structure. Through the thick darkness, they entered via a crumbling staircase and came upon a rabid, growling, crazed dog with filthy, matted fur. The dog was a large black-faced shepherd who paced and angrily guarded a staircase, which led to a lower level. The dog had been there for an exceedingly long time, alone and driven mad by a quest to protect me.

They passed the dog and entered a black staircase surrounded by peeling, moldy walls and headed down to a lower level. They came upon a brightly colored nesting doll. It was the only color in a sea of darkness. The guide led Wendy to see that a part of me was kept in the innermost layer of the doll. Wendy scooped up the figure and headed up the stairs and out toward the crumbling steps. The dog followed. As they departed, the dark landscape and crumbling hotel were replaced with an ancient grandmother tree, strong and powerful, with a thick trunk and deep roots. The nesting doll was placed at the base of the tree. The dog appeared beside it, protecting it still, but angry, scared, and worried at what was happening. A female jaguar appeared from around the back of the large tree trunk and immediately consumed the dog. A small girl with dirty, matted hair and worn clothing appeared in its place. She wore a necklace with three or four words on it. The jaguar dismembered the girl's body and neatly arranged the parts on the grass next to the tree. A group of seven skeletons appeared, surrounded the parts, and performed a healing ceremony. A female falcon appeared, grasped the nesting doll, and flew high to the top of the ancient grandmother tree, where she placed it inside a perfectly built nest. The falcon removed the first layer of the nesting doll to reveal the second. At the same moment, in coordination with the second layer being revealed, the tree sprouted beautiful pink flowers throughout its branches. The falcon stood guard over the nest and its contents and conveyed the possibility of more layers being removed, which revealed sparkling lights within the pink flowers.

The first impression Wendy received was the feeling of "organized disorder." What took away my trust happened at a young age. Instead of falling apart, I figured out how to survive. Each challenge I faced was tucked nicely into my organized-disorder file cabinet. It was the illusion of having control, the opposite of the unpredictable early life I had. The dark landscape and cityscape replaced the usual natural-landscape setting Wendy normally experiences. I explained to Wendy the experience I had in the third grade involving the dog that attacked me. It resembled the one who appeared in the lower world. Wendy thought I took the form of the dog, which represented my efforts to protect myself after losing my trust and vulnerability.

Wendy described the jaguar as "big medicine" when deep healing was required. She read from a book entitled *Animal Speak* by Ted Andrews, which described its attributes, and explained why animal spirit guides come into our lives.

On that day, jaguar and falcon supported me on my journey. I can continue to call on them.

Wendy explained more about how soul loss occurs when faced with the extreme suffering experienced during a shocking physical or emotional trauma.

A part of our soul or life force leaves the body to endure and survive the encounter. It is a natural, built-in self-preservation response, which occurs without any known effort. In shamanism, it is believed that the part of the disengaged soul goes to the dreamtime, or non-ordinary reality. Not knowing the traumatic event is over, the soul part will wait there until reestablished and reintegrated.

After reflecting on the shamanic healing session for a few months, I returned to Wendy for a soul-retrieval session. We again discussed in detail the moments of my life when I experienced significant trauma and resulting soul loss.

Although soul loss happens in order for you to survive these types of encounters, as life goes on, a stagnant feeling of loss persists. It is a feeling of something missing in your life, but you can't identify what the loss is exactly. But you know something is gone. This shows up in the form of anxiety, depression, addiction, loss of creativity, and an overall feeling of being disconnected. You are, in a sense, stuck in the moment of trauma forever. This can also lead to the development of illness and disease within the body. Until these soul parts are integrated back into your energy body, it is hard to fully process and heal from the events leading to the soul loss.

The lost soul part is kept in a pristine state, and when found, it returns a brilliant part of your soul, restoring your health, natural essence, and uniqueness. Like a midwife, a shaman can help you give birth—not to a child but to your true self. It sounds simple, but it will not happen unless you determinedly do the work needed to mend the effects of trauma, integrate the found soul parts, and recover your authentic self. I was more than willing.

The session began with the intoxicating mix of sage, drums, rattling, and whistling. When completed, Wendy explained how the whale shaman, a soul-retrieval-helper spirit in the form of a Pacific Northwestern native, emerged from the ocean wearing a loincloth and carrying a small wooden whale, which featured a mouth that opens to collect the lost soul parts. He joined her to begin the journey.

In the middle of a field of grass stood one perfectly formed daisy. This daisy represented me between the ages of one and four; it represented my potential. Lying alongside the daisy was a worn teddy bear, which provided comfort during my young life; it represented safety. I started out in life in the clutches of the highest sense of betrayal, which resulted in fear, lack of trust, and the loss of a sense of security. The daisy, along with the worn teddy bear, were retrieved.

A fawn appeared, which represented the period of ages seven and eight. The fawn represented innocence and the loss of it. The fawn followed them and was also retrieved.

Wendy and the whale shaman approached a young girl, between the ages of eleven and twelve, hiding on the side of a washing machine, knees pulled up to her chest and her head buried in her folded arms. She was hiding and reluctant to come out.

She did not want to stay there, but she had nowhere else to go. She was frightened and would not look up until Wendy told her the police were on their way. They needed her help to catch the man who did this to her so he would be punished and not be able to hurt anyone else. She immediately stood to join them and was retrieved. The limited amount of innocence, safety, and potential I had left was taken in the rectory. This was the most traumatic experience and led to the loss of the largest part of my soul and nearly the loss of my life.

The last and unexpected part collected, which was stuck in an unending horror, was the woman standing on the ferryboat staring at a smoke-filled black sky and cityscape burning in front of her eyes.

During our conversations where I informed Wendy about the details of what had happened to me, I did not embellish or include anything but the core facts. The teddy bear she mentioned was one I had for years as a small child. His name was Sam. He was given to me by an aunt and was practically glued to me for years. I wrote a story about him in the third grade.

Welcoming and integrating the retrieved soul parts is a restoration of your authentic self. When I did so, several emotions appeared and settled in, becoming smoother as I made space for being more grounded and balanced. The return of missing soul parts is also the return of the energies they left with. Integrating these stolen pieces of me brought back the ability to remember, but this time with sovereignty over the pain, understanding that these memories were the facts I needed to know in order to be freed from them. Another part of integration is the process of gathering photos from the time of the soul loss. I gathered a few, but looking into my childhood eyes was exceedingly difficult, and I could not muster more than a few seconds of trying. I prepared a folder to store them in until I was ready.

That night I had a dream. I felt myself in a tiny body. I was a toddler, around three years old. I was lying down; someone was behind me holding me down. I was struggling to break free; my arm came loose, and my finger went straight into the nostril of the person behind me. I felt absolute terror and woke myself. This was the first time I felt myself in my child body, and it would not be the last. It took a long time to recover and to get back to sleep. When I did, I returned to the same vision, but this time I was walking along a couch, stepping on the cushions and holding on to the back. A person was sitting in a chair next to the couch. I experienced a feeling of terror that I could not bear and woke myself again.

Much like I went on to study Reiki with Jean, my intense interest in this work led me to further explore shamanism by taking classes with Wendy. My sessions with her helped me to learn how I had to get out of my head before I could perceive with my heart and allow the ability of awareness to flow freely. I was ready to do a deep dive into shamanic work.

I returned in three months for my next healing session. Before the session officially started, Wendy felt the fiery bits of anger spiraling deep inside me. We discussed how the anger I carried was powerful and should be addressed.

The spirit helpers opened the healing session by bringing my dream body into harmony. Wendy explained that they were a group of twelve who specifically did this work. They did not look human, and as they surrounded my dream body, they used their voices to match the disharmony within, which at first was dissonant but then bended and formed into perfect harmony. Once in harmony, it was easier for Wendy to perceive. I mentioned the dreams and how they absolutely terrified me. I knew they were glimpses into what had happened to me. Wendy perceived how the dreams made the anger I had kept quiet inside boil up to the surface. I had quietly held this rage for my entire life, unassumingly, and now that this journey had taken me to this place of realization, it was boiling over in order to be released and healed.

The helpers led Wendy to a burned-out landscape still smoldering with small, scattered fires burning. It was completely charred with no greenery. A young version of me, around sixteen years old, lived in this landscape. She had a black Mohawk, wore old, beat-up leathers, and carried a flamethrower. The spirit helpers explained this was the warrior. She operated from a place of fierce anger, which did not serve me. She had the role of warrior, but in the negative expression of coercion. She was furious and strongly guarded. The helping spirits approached her. To try and connect, they offered the spirit of the stag to be in service to her.

The stag had a large rack of antlers, the picture of grace and strength, but from a place of vigor and leadership. The stag merged and took up residence in my dream body. He pulled her to the side, while the spirit helpers cleared out and removed the burned-out landscape and replaced it with a new one. The amount of energy it took for her to keep up the anger and be the protector was exhausting. She was on guard all the time with no rest. She was relieved and almost hypnotized by the stag. She had been alone for a long time and was glad to have help. The stag removed her heart, which was bandaged, wrapped many times around. Each time a new wound appeared, it would be wrapped again. The stag ate her heart and offered her a piece of his, which was filled with compassion and peace.

A large orange-and-black spotted butterfly appeared and wrapped her in a cocoon. The landscape became misty. When the cocoon opened, the landscape cleared and revealed a stone circle, surrounded by thick greenery with a mist hovering above it. Upon stepping out of the cocoon, the young girl appeared to be in her early twenties and much softer. The black Mohawk was replaced with a long braid down her back, and she wore a deerskin dress and had yellow butterfly tattoos around her neck, with one in the center at the fifth chakra. The stag stood with her, as did the butterfly. She was not alone any longer.

As a young child, I took on the role of the victim, but as I matured, I became a warrior. Although my silence kept me steeped in the negative expression of unseen anger, of which I was the byproduct, I have now gently moved into the positive expression of strength.

In shamanism, the role of warrior has two elements: the negative expression of coercion and the positive expression of persuasion.

Wendy concluded by saying, "You must use your voice, use your story, use your writing, and have unending compassion for yourself. Spend time in nature as much as you can. You must find the feeling of safety."

I had never felt completely safe in my entire life and wondered if I ever might be able to find that sense of peace.

Chapter Thirteen

QUANTUM LEAP

I found myself on a train. It was a large steam locomotive, black with red trim and only two cars long. I was comfortably lying on my side with my head resting on ornate silk pillows. The pillows were as cozy as they were opulent. My cat, Ravi, who had passed away many years earlier, was lying under my chin and I was petting him behind his ears. A woman was standing nearby and asked if I was comfortable. From my position, I could see into the first car, where a tall man dressed in a conductor's uniform stood. He wore a railroad cap with a shiny black visor and had many badges and pins affixed to his jacket. He busily moved various levers up and down, preparing to move the train. His left index finger became the focal point as it moved in slow motion toward a large red button on the dashboard. As he reached the space above the button, he stopped and hovered over it.

With his finger hanging in the air, he turned toward me, smiled, and asked, "Are you ready for your next adventure?"

It was six months past Mother's confession, which still clung to me like the putrid spray of a skunk I would never be able to wash off. I remained consumed with those unbearable words.

By fall, the years-old, on-and-off, inexplicable pelvic pain reared its ugly head again. The pain was so great, I went to the emergency room expecting a terrible diagnosis, but after many expensive tests, as usual, nothing was revealed. It was the first time the symptoms had arisen in over two years. My investigation into what happened to me during my childhood was well underway, and I continued learning new information and disturbing details. I knew the pelvic pain was related to the trauma I experienced, but I thought I was making enough progress on my journey of healing to keep it at bay. Yet here it was again. During a follow-up to review the useless test results, I told the truth of my history to my primary care doctor. It was the first time I had revealed the truth in this type of setting. It led her to recommend I see a friend who was an energy healer. I made an appointment right away. My wounds were deep and, in some ways, had become deeper in the last year as I had learned more about what happened.

Living in past wounds is what keeps us trapped and obstructs our ability to move forward. Further assistance in healing them is valuable and essential.

Upon meeting Jaime Pransky and receiving an introduction to Brennan Healing Science, it was instantly clear that I was marching into the next important phase of my journey . . . my next adventure.

In our first meeting, summarizing my story and my work of the past three years felt like a daunting task, but when I spoke, the information tenderly emerged in a detailed and passionate way. I held more authority over my story than I had in the past, although it was still grueling to disclose. Jaime listened intently. Her eyes focused on mine as we sat in a room that felt familiar and comfortable. I had a strong knowing it was a significant encounter, and I quickly settled into the flow of our work together.

Prior to meeting Jaime, I had never heard of Brennan Healing Science, but simply upon hearing the words spoken, I received validation through the familiar bursts of energy that purposely appeared to aid in the acknowledgment of moments of importance. Because of my familiarity and work thus far with Reiki and shamanic healing, Jaime explained the Brennan method as we went along, so I could have a deeper perception of its process.

Brennan Healing Science,[12] developed by Dr. Barbara Ann Brennan, a former NASA physicist who dedicated her life's research to exploring the human energy field and the expanses of human consciousness, is an in-depth, science-based, comprehensive approach to energy healing. She founded the Barbara Brennan School of Healing in 1982, a four-year accredited program with further opportunities for advanced studies and teacher training. Dr. Brennan's background served to bring a calculated scientific approach to her work. She authored several best-selling books, which I became avidly focused on.

Jaime and I met once a week. She delicately dug deeper than I previously had into the core parts of my story, focusing on the places where I needed to understand with further clarity the root cause and results of the suffering I experienced. Like when a doctor cleans out a wound to prevent infection so it can fully heal, this work further cleaned out the wounds on my soul and at the cellular level.

If wounds are not cleansed, they can fester and develop into a more serious condition.

From observing my energy field, Jaime perceived certain things I had not yet revealed to her, such as when she thanked me for staying here on earth.

Our first hands-on healing session brought about an incredible discovery that supported and broadened my approach to my work. Jaime began the healing session at the bottom of my feet, opposite the teachings of Reiki, which began at the top of the head. After a few minutes, she observed I had undergone a complete restoration of my hara line, sometimes known as a reincarnation in the same body (RSB).

The hara line is the line of communication between the soul and the personality. It is the foundation of our energy bodies and where our human energy system rests. It holds our life purpose. An RSB consists of dissolving the hara line and rebuilding a new one. The completion of the life task makes RSB a possibility, and an opportunity for evolution, while avoiding the stressful process of leaving a body and enduring another birth.

RSB is an organic process involving preparation, integration, and completion phases as the cells of the body adjust to the new vibrations. This process can last from less than a year to several years. The deep dive I took into my dark past, my intense healing and soul-retrieval work, and my search for the truth was surely the catalyst.

This process must have started when I spoke my truth for the first time after decades of silence. It also explained my frequent feelings of being disoriented. I did feel like a new person—still me but different. Although I still had work to do to completely revitalize my authentic self, I was restored and felt like I had a clean slate to work with. Receiving this validation confirmed that the work I had been deeply engaged in was succeeding and I was on my way to realizing wholeness.

After the observation and conversation regarding the restored hara line, Jaime perceived the function of my chakra system, or lack thereof, advising me that the lower three chakras—the root, the sacral, and the solar plexus—were completely shut down, which was consistent with experiences of sexual trauma and deep relational betrayal. To restore vitality to these areas, Jaime explained she would perform a chelation.

The word "chelation" is derived from a Greek word that means "to claw." The purpose of chelation is to drag out deep-rooted, unresponsive energy and replace it with pure, restored, and responsive energy.

A strong feeling of nausea rose in my solar plexus chakra and lasted for several days. This was the most wounded of the damaged lower three chakras.

The solar plexus chakra contains the energy of our relationship with the self and connectedness to others. It is intricately linked with the emotions and perception of safety and belonging. It is the border between the heart chakra and beyond.

Mine was completely closed off. The blocked solar plexus chakra was what created a disconnect to the feeling of belonging in the world, to the sense of feeling safe, and to my overall greater purpose. The nausea made that disconnect explicitly clear.

My writing was in the note-taking stage in my journal, in piles of handwritten notes on stickies and junk mail, and in typed notes on my phone. I gathered and cataloged all the information I was receiving, remembering, and uncovering faithfully and precisely. Throughout a methodical increase in my dedication to this work, my writing progressed to a more orderly style, and I shaped the piles into form and assembled each detail into a time line. As my work unfolded, it became imperative for me to tell my story, and although it gave me an uneasy feeling due to its salacious content and deeply personal nature, it conveyed a feeling of intense importance. The significance of this work propelled me forward. I found the time to dedicate to writing each day, whether it was for two minutes or two hours.

The practitioner-client relationship I formed with Jaime effortlessly evolved to become a friendship and a mentor-mentee bond. I was intensely interested in Brennan Healing Science, and Jaime served as my entrance into learning more about this method of energy healing. We started with a deep dive into the chakra system and related levels of the human energy field. My prior work and basic understanding of these subjects was a helpful prerequisite, and using myself as the subject was an effective approach.

Starting at the root chakra, we focused on grounding techniques to help regulate my trauma-informed emotions of instinct, survival, and safety. I had been habitually ungrounded and untethered, hovering inches above the ground for my entire life, until discovering my work with Reiki and shamanism, when I remedied this disconnection and disassociation to my body. Thereafter, our sessions focused on the next chakra and the methods to heal and reenergize its life force. I spent several weeks on each, integrating the work into every aspect of my life.

Appearing across many traditions and cultures with varying degrees of specifics, the primary influence that defines the chakra system remains the Hindu tradition and teachings. The word "chakra" derives from a Sanskrit word meaning "wheel of light." Located along the main branch of the nervous system, these "wheels" serve as energy collectors and transmitters, connecting our physical, emotional, mental, and spiritual bodies through the *nadis*, a network of energy channels. Chakras are perceived as circular vortices in a conical shape affiliated with a color, a sound, an element, and a lotus flower, each with a specific number of petals. There are seven main chakras that ascend along the base of the spine to the top of the head, each connected to a particular area of the endocrine and nervous systems. Each chakra performs its own unique functions within these levels and, when they are fully operating in unison, creates a healthy life force energy that supports our physical, emotional, mental, and spiritual health.

There are some similarities yet many differences between the practices of Reiki and Brennan Healing Science. Both are hands-on healing methods that use the chakra system and meridians as position points, but they channel energy using differing hand placements and sequences. Reiki has seen widespread popularity and use due to its convenient learning model and user-friendliness. It is learned in easily accessible short courses.

Brennan Healing Science is taught as an intensive four-year program spanning over two thousand hours with specific and rigorous requirements. It is a deep commitment personally and financially with many benefits and esteemed credentials.

I was so grateful to have my work with Jaime and the invaluable chance to learn from her directly and by studying the Brennan Healing Science books. Combined with my existing work, it all started to take form, propelling me forward further into the world of energy medicine.

The core teaching of practitioners in any healing practice is to bring to the student deep personal development and an awakening of consciousness, which allows for the ability of the student to be a clear and present energy channel. What is most important in any focused healing work, as practitioner, client, or student, is our own personal inner work. We are our own healers. If you leave it up to a practitioner of any background to solely heal you without further effort on your part, it will never happen. The work of healing is deeply personal.

With prompts and guidance from each of the healing methods I found myself entrenched in, combining approaches from each served as my personal healing toolbox.

Having the right mentors is essential for guidance and learning, but having a personal connection is vital and at the heart of healing.

The nature of my dreams took on a new complexity. I realized these dreams had become a method of receiving information and keys to insight. I wrote everything down as soon as I awakened.

I call these dreams "vision dreams." They are different than lucid dreaming, which also happens to me often. In those, I am aware I am dreaming but able to control my actions and lead the direction of the dream. These vision dreams are different, striking, and memorable without effort, and all have a telepathic nature. They articulate a deeply personal affirmation and certainty.

A few nights before my birthday, I had a vision dream and woke knowing I would be receiving a call with the news that Mother had passed. In the dream, I was surrounded by a group of tall shadowy figures. I felt safe, not frightened. In the next moment, I was with a group of eighteen people. We waited for the results of a particularly important matter. There was much excitement, music, and dancing. It was a celebration. I sat on a ledge close to others whose faces I could not make out, with my legs dangling and swaying back and forth. Then, everyone started cheering excitedly. The person to my right turned toward me and said, "All of your hard work has paid off!" Everyone was smiling and happy.

I woke startled. I quickly wrote a summary of the dream in my journal. A short time later, as I prepared coffee, the phone rang, and a burst of energy shot from the bottom of my feet to the top of my head. I knew it was the call to inform me of Mother's passing.

After the conversation, I revisited the dream again. I understood the shadowy figures were my guides. They held me in safety as my ancestors waited for her. How do I mourn for someone who stole the most precious things from me—my innocence, my sense of safety—and instead handed me a life sentence of shame and fear? She altered my unformed brain to try and wipe the memories, albeit temporarily, and, when the obvious reactive problems arose, she made me believe something was wrong with me. For so long, I hoped and dreamed she would magically transform into the mother I needed so badly, but she never did. The status quo, however dysfunctional, was kept. As much as I tried to please her, I only compromised myself. There was a deep individual and personalized aloneness stemming from this type of trauma, not just for me but for her as well. She projected her pain with impunity onto me. Her failures and flaws were mine too. This helped me to understand ancestral trauma and fully accept and be grateful for the empathy and compassion I had found to bring her to Vermont. I would have never learned the truth, but, more importantly, I never wanted to lose those qualities.

Perhaps feeling only relief after the passing of one's mother is worse than the normal or standard grief one should feel upon losing what is typically the most significant connection to another human being.

Assuming the role was filled by someone who was loving and at the least performed even the basic tasks a mother should, this loss would garner an appropriate amount of grieving. While she did not gift me with the customary affections of motherly love and protection, she did unwittingly gift me with raging stoicism and courage.

I briefly considered the thought that I should cry, but not one tear fell. Her miserable, pain-soaked, and forfeited life was over. In that one single moment, an enormous weight had been lifted from me. I stood and, for the first time, felt the sturdy and solid ground beneath my feet.

As fall approached, I met with Celine again. I had completed months of research and personal healing work. I was ready to learn further information spirit might provide. This time I had specific questions for my parents, who both were now crossed over.

Celine began. "A female energy came right through saying she is like dust in the wind now. What is your question for her?"

Knowing it was Mother, I said, "I want to know who abused her."

"It was Giovanni. He was an incredibly angry, sick, tortured, and confused man who took out his rage on women, children, and even pets. She is showing me three steps on the side of a house. There is a clothesline, a large tree, and water. There is significance to the water. Those three steps lead somewhere central to this story. He wore a baseball cap. He had dark hair that he pushed back as he put the cap on. I see him tying his fancy black shoes. He is older, but not much, wearing a striped shirt, younger man's clothing. Italians were considered Black at this time in history, and this made him angry. I see beans in a cast-iron pan. He did not like beans, but there was no other food."

Giovanni was a relative. I was sick to my stomach. I did not want to believe what I heard. The area she described was the side yard of our apartment building with three steps leading inside. I asked, "Was he the one who coerced her into abusing me?"

"Yes, other men did too. She prepared you for them, groomed you. You were between two and three years old. She passed down her suffering. Remember, this happens through generations."

I held back tears, intense anger, and a strong feeling of nausea. "Did this begin when my father left?"

Celine replied, "Yes. I can see him. He stands by the tree in the backyard. He was a quiet man, a kind man. The men pushed him out. They thought he was gay because he was caring and treated women with respect. He knew your mother was abused and tried to help. He was the opposite of them, and they hated him for it. He is giving me a name . . . Silvio. Something happened here, something connected to the water, and he was threatened with a knife by this person. He thought he would be murdered or at least badly hurt."

I asked about the name that had been swirling in my mind for so long. "Who is The Captain?"

"He had power over the family, like he was in charge."

I asked what I already knew. "Was I given to him for money?"

"Yes. I keep getting something about water. It is something significant. Your mother is saying, 'It is over now.' She sends you love and hopes for understanding. There are no excuses, but there were reasons. She offers daisies and a heart and says it is not necessary to prove your worth. You are worthy. She never felt worthy."

Spirit was pulling away. I had so many more questions, but they would have to wait until next time. This conversation was a treasure trove of information. It was sickening and exhilarating at the same time. I knew I was uncovering something more sinister than I could have ever anticipated.

A pattern of matched and coordinated information was emerging from each of my helpers, none of whom had any contact with the others. My own intuitive knowings and vision dreams added to the pattern of a synchronous flow, which met on various points and continued shaping the narrative of the puzzle I was diligently piecing together. I noticed how each of my helpers naturally flowed into my life at the precise moments they were needed, and I was ready.

The next helper who entered the story would assist in uncovering a tsunami of information, linking the pieces of existing details to newly revealed ones and forging a path toward the completion of the sordid puzzle I had been assembling. I was wholly engaged in the importance and need to further validate my findings to the best of my ability.

Working with more than one medium or clairvoyant is beneficial when trying to obtain and validate patterns of information. All have different ways of communicating with spirit. The conversations I was about to step into would send me plummeting from a great height. Sometimes I fell helplessly, slamming against jagged rocks, which left cavernous puncture wounds, bumps, and bruises along the way. Yet sometimes I fell gracefully and with purpose, collecting the scattered pieces of me and reshaping the narrative of my story.

Gerard Aviti, a medium from my hometown of Staten Island, was recommended to me by Michele. At the beginning of my journey, Michele had prompted me to explore Reiki. This time, her prompt would lead to the explosive conclusion of my investigation.

Chapter Fourteen

THE HOUSE
OF SECRETS

After pleasant introductions, Gerard provided his background information and details about how he worked as a medium. During sessions, he scribbled on a pad to focus his mind and hear spirit clearly. Sometimes he was guided to write down certain words or phrases. Gerard instructed me to focus on who I would like to communicate with and to give them permission to speak with him. I had prepared for this session by reviewing my notes, creating a time line of events, and composing questions I hoped to get answers to. I called on the two people who knew everything and had the deepest connection to me: my parents.

"A male energy and a female energy are here—Mom and Dad," Gerard said. "Both sets of grandparents are here, and another female energy, an aunt. The mother energy is strong. I am feeling breathing problems. Is this how she passed? My head hurts, too, which usually means there is a form of dementia." He closed his eyes and continued, "She said dementia was a blessing for her, a gift. She is grateful for you bringing her to the facility. She had three children, wait . . . there is more. A few more."

Gerard's opening words provided validation, and I had immediate confidence in his ability. Although I did not call them, both my paternal and maternal grandparents were present, along with my aunt, whom I had previously communicated with during my second reading with Celine. I never knew my paternal grandparents, but, as Gerard explained, they know me, they are with me, and they watch over me. *Better late than never, I guess.*

Gerard struggled and was visibly uncomfortable. He squirmed in his chair. Since he did not know anything about me, I told him a simple, basic background, without detail but enough to convey it was a dark, tragic, and sad history, and I told him that the reason for my reading today was to validate and acquire further information. He looked relieved. I was sure if he was receiving information that he knew would be shocking to his client, he might hesitate to pass it on. I did not know anything about the ethics of mediumship, but as in any therapeutic profession, I assumed there were basic values and standards to abide by. I did appreciate what I perceived as his instinct to protect me.

"There were many more unwanted pregnancies; they were the result of abuse. She kept them hidden. She was beaten—physically, emotionally, verbally, and sexually. I am getting a male relative energy as an abuser. He ruined many lives. She is concerned and wants you to be careful with what you are uncovering. There are many implications. She was not the only one. He left behind a trail of bodies, and he was not the only one who did. There were several more abusers in the community. The person you are thinking of now is not ready to remember. It will be a few more years, and when it happens, it will be intense. He will need support. He is not built like you. You became a warrior; he is still a victim. She is showing me the scales of justice and a priest. Do you know why?"

I replied, "I am involved in a lawsuit against the Archdiocese of New York and others."

"Oh, that explains the priest! She says, 'Go get 'em.' Your aunt adds how they have understanding now and would do things differently if they had a second chance. She calls you a sacrificial lamb. Your father is apologizing for leaving you there. He thought, or he convinced himself to think, you would be all right. He is deeply sorry for what happened after he left. He is saying, 'I'm sorry.'"

Gerard scanned in front of him. He said, "He is not here. Why?" His chin lifted and he raised his eyebrows as if he was listening. "The punishment fits the crime. Your mother's first abuser is not here because he is an earthbound spirit. He has been stuck since his passing."

Gerard explained further. "Earthbound spirits are the souls who have not crossed over after leaving their physical bodies for any number of reasons. Sometimes, they have simply lost their way or succumbed to the denial of their own death. They remain in an often-frustrating, temporary state. Sometimes a soul remains through guilt of bad behavior and a fear of punishment for their wrongdoings. They are stuck in an in-between place. Spirits who have crossed become enlightened and shed the heavier human base of emotions. They see the mistakes they made and try to rectify them. They learn their lessons. Many earthbound spirits are not willing to see the mistakes they made and do not attempt to rectify or learn from them."

Gerard's validating statements matched the pattern of information I previously received from Celine, specifically that it was a male relative who was Mother's first abuser. I asked Gerard if I could ask a question of my mother. He nodded.

I asked, "Who is The Captain?"

"She does not want to talk about this." He closed his eyes and softly said, "That's not good enough." His light started to flicker several times, and the mute button was activated on the video conference. I saw a flash of light out of the corner of my right eye. Gerard unmuted but as soon as he spoke, the mute button was activated again.

Over the last few years, I had become accustomed to these flashes of light, words spoken in the middle of the night, and the shadows of visitors that disappeared in an instant. I knew this question was a crucial part of the story that I needed an answer to. The name The Captain had never left my memory since childhood.

Gerard pressed the unmute button again, and with hesitancy and obvious discomfort he said in a quiet voice, "I see words . . ." In a sad tone he said, "Sex trade. An underworld existed in your community, and The Captain had power in it. You, among many others, were a victim of this group. Your mother is concerned and worried about you exposing this. There could be much pushback, and she is worried about the implications you may have to deal with. She is saying to keep writing—write the book—but be careful." He directed his question to me. "Are you writing a book?"

I replied, "Yes, I am."

Gerard excitedly said, "This book is your soul purpose! It is bringing injustice to light and stopping the pattern of silence in the lineage. Whether it is published or not, it will still achieve this. Your frequency is extremely high."

I told Gerard I had been studying energy medicine for the last few years, from Reiki to shamanism and currently Brennan Healing Science.

He smiled. "You will continue to grow as a healer. More will come from this book; your work will be to help others. Along the way, do not forget to take care of yourself. You will be on a mission to help as many people as you can. You are a warrior for truth and justice."

After a few moments of quiet, Gerard mentioned that my maternal grandmother wanted to speak. She was often with me; I felt her presence.

He began, "She says, 'It has been in the blood for generations, molestation and abuse. I was a victim too. You broke the
cycle by speaking the truth. The ones who push back at you are
not the ones you need. There has been enough silence. You are
the voice of all the victims, and the light you shine will become
a beacon after the storm.'" With tears in his eyes, Gerard added,
"They all support you, some reluctantly, but you have their support. There will be some divine intervention. They are backing
away now, but your mother will have the last words. She said
she is sorry for not being strong, for failing you, for not being
the mother you needed. She loves you dearly. She was tortured,
mentally groomed to be a victim from a young age. She is
concerned for you and has much remorse, regret, shame, and
embarrassment."

Upon completing the call with Gerard, I sat quietly with
my eyes closed. I thanked my ancestors for showing up and for
providing the details I needed, as difficult as they were to hear.
It took time to organize my thoughts. The call confirmed who
Mother's initial abuser was and what role The Captain played in
our story. I felt a deep feeling of relief yet also a deep sadness. I
was crushed by the lurid details but also had the opposite feeling
of empowerment, which only truth could give. This conversation explained Mother more thoroughly. Before, I could only
see her shortcomings and deficiencies as a person and a parent,
but now I knew she was also a victim. When I stood to stretch
my body and breathe, a strong energy raced up my legs through
my torso to the top of my head. I felt the familiar soft pressure
of energy bodies around me, my spirit guide on my right, my
grandmother on my left, as they always were. I knew I had to
take it slow, but I anxiously counted the days until my next
meeting with Gerard.

Later in the afternoon, I was walking my dog around the
neighborhood, as I did every day, filling Michele in on the details.

A small voice from behind me said, "Can I pet your dog?"

A tiny little girl, two or three years old, was sitting on a swing in her front yard along with people who I assumed were her grandparents. I asked Michele to hold. The little girl jumped from the swing and happily skipped to us to pet my dog. I bent to get to her height.

I said hello and introduced myself and my dog. "My dog loves to make new friends. What is your name?"

She softly replied, "Grace." She had dark-blonde hair and big hazel eyes. She wore a cute outfit with unicorns and rainbows. She gently moved her tiny hand across the top of my dog's head and smiled.

"How old are you?"

She held up her closed fist and slowly pulled up three fingers, one at a time, concentrating on each one and counting along. "I'm three." She smiled and looked right into my eyes, which filled with tears. Her eyes were pure innocence. A wave of emotion took over. I needed to leave before I burst.

"I need to get going," I said, and I waved goodbye. I was flooded with sadness. Michele, hearing my voice crack, talked me through it.

"It's okay. Let it out. You must let it out. I'm here for you."

When I was looking at Grace, I felt like I was looking at myself; the color of her hair and her eyes were identical to mine. For the first time, I connected to how terrified I must have been as a child, how helpless and unable to understand what was happening to me and around me. I had not cried much during my time of remembering, investigating, and wondering, even with the new information I was receiving. It felt good to finally release the sadness.

Grace was there for a reason—to remind me to find grace within myself during the uncovering of this story . . . to access and connect to the little girl inside of me and let her know she was safe now.

Grace teaches us to let go of things we have no control over and to trust that if we are open to finding our way through, we do not need to have control, only an understanding of flow. Grace does not listen to self-doubts and does not keep score. Grace is a feeling of acceptance. Grace is being present. I knew I needed to surrender to and let grace guide me through the uncovering of this story without suffering but with understanding and an unfailing need for the truth. I knew I needed to allow it to carry me through each phase of discovery, loving myself completely, and finding my way toward forgiveness for what seemed like unforgivable actions.

As I moved forward, I had to try to mourn what had been lost and yet also be grateful for the moments of resilience I was fortunate to have, which saved me from complete collapse. Now, I was officially obsessed with the story of what happened, not solely to me but to Mother, my family, my ancestors, my friends, and my community. There could no longer be silence about what happened—no more lies, no more cover-ups. Only understanding, only truth.

It had been exactly one month since our first session. I anxiously waited for Gerard to join our video conference. As I stared at the screen, I prepared myself by reviewing my journal entries and the notes from the previous session. I had no specific questions. I planned to let it flow as it would. My heart beat faster as soon as Gerard appeared on the screen. We had a pleasant chat before getting to the task at hand.

He began, "A female energy is here—a mother energy; a male energy is here—a father energy; both sets of grandparents are here, and another female energy—your aunt is here. We have the same group as our last time together. The mother energy is stronger than last time. Your grandmother is standing right next to her in a protective stance. She is protecting you. She loves you so much. Your aunt is stepping forward. She is apologizing. She sends her deep apologies to you."

Gerard lowered his head and closed his eyes for a moment before he continued. "Your aunt is showing me a basement with wood-paneled walls. I'm sorry to describe it like this, but it is like a sex dungeon. She is saying this was one of two locations. One place was for staging, grooming, and one place for the acts. I see a camera. There was filming and photographs taken. One location does not exist anymore, and the other does."

"A network operated this ring. It contained people in positions of authority. The others involved were perverse or weak and manipulated. There were many layers. Your aunt is showing me a teenager."

Without hesitation, I had a strong knowing it was The Teenager who had molested me in our apartment while I was home alone after school. I closed my eyes and saw his face in my mind, exactly as he looked as he knelt in front of me as I sat on the couch. I did not mention what I was thinking to Gerard, who added that The Teenager was a victim of this network too.

I said, "I may know the real name of The Captain."

Gerard was scribbling on his pad. He lifted it toward the screen to show he had written down the first four letters of The Captain's last name. "Your aunt confirmed, yes, it is him. He was born sick, a sociopath with no emotions. He saw children as objects. He was the one who took the photos and films. She is telling me he kept trophies. He always kept something from the abused children, like a barrette or underwear. When he died, someone found everything and burned it all. He is also earthbound and will remain so for a long time."

I explained to Gerard that since our last session, fragments of memories had surfaced that took on a new meaning. "I remember the house of The Captain, specifically a garden. I had remembered this vaguely my entire life, but it is much clearer now. On

Google Maps, I found the house and an owner name. Michele helped me do some digging. She found an article from the late 1980s in a local newspaper about a young woman with the same last name who survived an attempted suicide."

Gerard said, "She was a victim too; she has knowledge of everything. Your aunt is showing The Captain in a car with no brakes and a kid at the bottom. He was a serial child abuser in the community and in his own family. His house was a house of horrors; this might be the second location."

After a few moments of scribbling on his notepad, Gerard resumed. "Your aunt is showing me a man in a business suit sitting at a bar. She is saying . . . 'involved.'"

During my investigating, I'd also searched the property records of the bar, and found the owner's name. I drew a check next to his name in my time line as Gerard continued.

"The people running this child-abuse ring designed it and had a formula. They planned who they chose, how and what and where they did it, and how they covered it up. As I said, there were people in positions of authority." Gerard looked disgusted, a look that matched my own.

"Was there a suspicious death? I am given a head injury. It was an adult. There was a cover-up, and they made it look like natural causes. There were three men involved. Your mother is saying to be careful with this. You are going to find out more about this soon."

I was aware of a suspicious death but had no details. I added this to my list of items to explore. "I need to address my experience of sexual assault with The Priests. Only scattered pieces of my memory remained intact over the years, but ever since I decided to file a lawsuit, I have tried my best to be clear about what I remember. Was it only one of the two priests who were there?"

Gerard replied, "No, your aunt is showing me another priest

with him. They are at the altar in full vestments; one outranks the other. She is saying it was both."

When I gave my statement to my attorney, I listed the second priest as a potential accomplice, even though I felt strongly he was more involved. Here was another validation and a reminder to listen to my intuition.

I mentioned Sister Mary Darcy, who I firmly believed handpicked the children for abuse.

Gerard saw her and described her as "evil, wicked, and with black eyes." He compared her appearance to that of a character in the horror movie *The Nun*.

"She menacingly appeared before me in a dream a few months ago. I attacked her with powerful energy. I was wearing a red tank top."

He replied, "You took your power she was holding back. Red is believed to ward off evil spirits. I do not use the words 'evil' and 'wicked' lightly, but this is the only way to describe her."

I felt a pull in the energy around me. Spirit was backing away. Although I did not have the same gifts as Gerard, I did sense their presence enough to know the end of our time together was approaching.

Gerard finished with, "They don't want to overwhelm you with information, not because they think you can't handle it, but because you will need the time to write and investigate the story piece by piece. They have many regrets about how they wronged you so badly in life. They want this to be an opportunity to help you. They will give you all the information you need in time. Your passion is the truth. You are awake and aware; the others are blissfully ignorant."

I stared at the black screen of my laptop with my mind fixated on one question: Did any physical evidence, the photos or videos, made by The Captain still exist?

As intensely as I was focused on this investigation and research, I had to slow down so I did not miss any important details. Sixty days later, I met with Gerard for our third session together. After a friendly conversation about the holidays and the excitement of starting a new year amid the uncertainty of the pandemic we'd been living with for almost two years, Gerard explained that during his meditation before our call, he had a lump in his throat, which meant either that spirit did not want to talk or that one entity was trying to stop the conversation from happening. I guessed the latter, considering the subject. We did our usual connection and, thankfully, everything proceeded smoothly.

He began, "A mother energy, an aunt energy, a father energy . . . and, after a long pause . . . I am hearing a perpetrator is here. It is The Captain. My guide will keep a tight rein on him. His soul has not crossed over. He thinks he is smarter than everyone. He is still full of himself. Your mother and your aunt dragged him here. They want him to answer for what he's done. They have crossed over. They are atoning. He is another story. He is used to calling the shots, and when things don't go his way, he gets angry. He says he had people under him, three in total. Your mother said to him, 'This is going to help your soul,' and he arrogantly replied, 'I don't need any help.'"

Gerard explained how spirits who held narcissistic, domineering power in their human lives and refused to atone and grow in their spiritual lives attempt to wield the same power in the spirit world, always to their greatest detriment.

I wrote the word "here" next to The Captain/main perpetrator listed in the top box of a hierarchical chart I drew in my journal. The box connected to a line below that split into three arrows pointing to three more boxes. Only two out of the three contained names. The first one was Giovanni, Mother's abuser. The second was The Business Man. The third was blank with a small question mark in the upper right corner, leaving space for the name I had hoped to fill in during this session.

Gerard sensed another male and female energy present.

I said, "I called in two spirits, one male and one female, both family members whom we have not spoken with yet but who I know will have answers."

Gerard sensed the male spirit, but not the female spirit, was afraid of The Captain and hung back a bit. He added, "Your mother and aunt are not afraid of him. Not anymore, anyway."

I asked Gerard, "Does the physical evidence, the photos or videos, still exist?"

Gerard said, "Things were constantly moving. The Captain made sure not to be sloppy. He kept his matters fluid. What he personally kept, he hid well. Remember, after his death evidence was found and destroyed. Your mother is telling me there is a box buried deep in a forgotten place. A place like an attic or basement. The people who have it do not know it is there, and even if they did find it, the items in the box would not be anything that would give any solid information. There is a notebook or ledger, but they never marked items with names; they used code and nicknames."

Gerard mentioned that spirit was showing him the book; he asked for them to open it. "It looks like Morse code or shorthand. This notebook is hidden in that box. It would be of great value to you for understanding the narrative but not clear enough to use as evidence. It might make sense to you but not to others."

I asked, "Where is it located?"

He replied, "Spirit is pulling toward a rural area. North. It is in the possession of a woman. She is a family member of The Captain, a daughter or female relative. The chance of you getting this is slim. This book is not the only path, though. The road you are walking on right now comes to a fork, with both ways leading to the same spot." Gerard sighed and added, "The Captain is getting agitated as we are talking about this."

"Was The Captain in the Mafia?

"Yes, but he wasn't a made person. He was a low-level associate. He thought he was higher in rank than he was and liked to make it seem he was to people outside of that world, but he was not looked kindly upon. They knew something was off about him. Mafia have a keen sense of pinpointing others' deviances, and they did not trust him. Your mother just said, 'Don't lose focus, it's a dead end.' As much as those people are horrible, this is something they would not engage in, and if they had known what was going on, they would have taken care of him. It's a piece of information and paints a broader picture, but it is not a key point to lead you where you need to go. It will pull you away from your path instead of bringing you closer."

Gerard asked, "Do you know if The Captain had a boat?"

"I'm not sure, but maybe that is why they called him The Captain."

Gerard said, "I am seeing a water connection to him, a fishing type of boat. Nothing happened on the boat, but I am being pulled to know there was a boat where they would go to be away and have privacy to talk about their plans. Remember, there was money involved here."

Then Gerard asked, "Did The Captain have siblings?"

I replied, "I'm not sure."

Gerard said, "Someone in his family may have been the owner of the boat. His family did not all follow the path he did. There were a few who knew and got involved, but most did not."

Gerard, curious about the two new spirits, stated, "The male is a bit younger and has a different feel. Do you think he was involved?"

I said, "I think he was a victim, which is why I called for him to be here. He suffered from years of heavy alcohol abuse. I always thought something bad happened to him."

Gerard confirmed, "He was a victim of the network and was

taken along for the ride. When he presents himself, it feels like he is stuck in time. He has crossed over, but the abuse was significant. His life stopped at that point. He struggled afterward. He lost his purpose, and it rippled through his life. It ripped him apart. He had many difficulties for many years. I sense his energy as kind and warmhearted. I have much sympathy for him."

Gerard asked about the female energy. "She has a much different feel."

"I called in Jane, the wife of Giovanni. Giovanni had been one of the three perpetrators under The Captain. Since learning Mother's history, I believed he was the thread that connected my family to this group.

Gerard took several moments in concentration and while still scribbling said, "She was involved; I think she is the third." He held up his pad, which showed a large number three, and continued speaking. "She is different and has darkness in her. Some were forced into it; some were afraid to get out of it; I think she enjoyed it. She was twisted. She held power in the group—approval power—just as strong as one of the men. If there is any thread to pull right now, it lies with her. She kept more secrets than The Captain, who fancied himself the boss of things, but she carries herself like she is the boss. She was instrumental in setting up and hiding abuse. She was the idea person. It came out of The Captain's mouth, but she was like the consigliere . . . devious, wicked. She was a person who sat back and watched the world burn. It came from her own childhood, which planted a dark seed that she ran with. For the others, it was a sexual perversion; for her it was control and power. I think she was devoid of any remorse, even now. She is earthbound also."

After a long pause, Gerard eventually resumed talking: "When connecting to both The Captain and Jane, I feel more remorse hidden in him than in her, and he doesn't have much to begin with. For him, there were times he couldn't resist, like a moth to a flame. For her, she was calculating. She could have stopped it, but she chose not to."

Gerard said, "Was there a fireplace or a brick wall in their home? There is something hidden in that house. I keep seeing stone or brick with papers buried behind or under it. After the papers were put there, it was sealed back up. I see letters, correspondence, and notes between the group, four or five pieces of paper. It was a hiding place. They all used code names, too, not only The Captain. Someone had a bird moniker."

Gerard asked if I had any more questions.

"I have a question about being in a car with my best friend and her mom when I was about ten years old. We sat in the back seat and her mom stopped to run into a store. The car was running, and when she left, I started to have an anxiety attack. I did not know what it was at the time, and I tried to cover it up by pretending I had to go to the bathroom. I could not sit still and was terrified, but I didn't know why. As soon as she returned to the car, I settled down. This remembrance has been recurringly popping into my thoughts recently, and I believe it is to lead me to discover the truth behind those feelings. To this day, I cannot sit comfortably in the back seat of a car. I am reminded how the body keeps the score." I braced myself. "Did something happen to me in the back seat of a car?"

"You don't remember?" He mentioned how he experienced a strong smell of sulfur, an acrid odor, as soon as I raised this topic. "They don't want you to know this, but yes, it happened twice. You were young, around three. When I see it playing out, they are careful with what to show me. I feel the car moving and you traveling somewhere before it parks. It was a male with short dark hair, thin, side part. He feels connected to The Captain. I want to say a cousin or someone close to him."

Throughout the process of uncovering what had happened, I tried to remain accepting of the painful information I had been intent on gathering. I was balanced and composed, thanks to my helpers, my healing practice, and my energy-medicine work. My demand for truth kept me focused. But at this moment, it all melted away and I found myself completely enraged.

I asked in a loud voice, "How did they take me away in a car? Did my mother simply give me to these people?"

"Your mother made herself unaware. She didn't want to believe it and was afraid to confront anyone because if she caused too much of a stink, she would have paid for it. She was as much a victim as she was a perpetrator. When it comes to her, there is no black-and-white, not like the others. I don't feel the evil in her, I feel fear. I feel the emotion of poverty, not enough food or money to pay bills. She talked herself into thinking everything was fine, she ignored it, she let it happen because she was also afraid for herself. It was either her or you."

There were many times throughout my life when I detested Mother but none more so than at that moment. I let my anger temporarily take me over. I needed to feel this rage. I wanted to not believe any of this, but each time I received a validation of my intuition, it made me doubt myself less. I wondered how much more heartbreaking information I might find through investigating this story. Some people had to have known what was going on, but not one person stepped up to help. As I reined in the anger and recovered, I reminded Gerard that in our second meeting, my aunt referred to me as a sacrificial lamb.

He agreed. "Your mother knows she should have thrown herself on the grenade."

Gerard lowered his head as he listened. "The younger male wants to talk, but Jane was holding him back before. They worked him over big-time; not only was he molested but they also involved him in a molestation. He said they made him do it. It was not you. It is what broke his will more than anything else. His molestation caused stress fractures, but it was the pressure of what they forced him to do that broke him. The girl was a bit younger or around the same age. It was not intercourse but touching. He did not want to do it, but they threatened him with violence. They made him do it, simply because someone wanted to watch. They liked playing around with people's innocence and ruining it."

Gerard mentioned how sometimes he holds on to information he has received until he gets a more complete picture or solid knowing, and he added, "A third location existed. Remember, they played the shell game. They believed they would not get caught if they kept it moving. This location was the home of someone who was above The Captain in this group. The Captain had a lot of control, but this person had more."

I said, "I've had dreams of being in a specific house in our neighborhood. Two startling dreams. I believe they are related to this person."

Gerard sought an answer and said, "Yes, absolutely; your mother says it is where everything started. She calls it 'The House of Secrets.' You still need to fill in a piece of the puzzle before you get here. I feel like you started at the end of the story and are working your way toward the beginning. There are still events to be put into place. I feel an older male connected to this place. The Captain didn't fear this older man; he respected him, which is unusual because I did not think it was an emotion he was capable of. He respects him like a father figure."

I quickly jot down "Old Man" in capital letters and drew a line on the page connecting him to the top box of the hierarchical chart, which contained the name The Captain. Gerard continued, "Your mother is policing what and how information is coming through, not so much to hide it but to make sure you don't overlook anything. As much as you are aware of, there is twice as much you are not, and only half of that you will learn. Some of it has been lost to time through death and destruction of records and property. But there is someone bigger. He is connected to this house and is the last one involved on a big scale. This house holds darkness. I keep hearing this was where it all started. Not just concerning you, but where this entire story started. This house is the focal point.

"Your mother is strong. She pulled these spirits through and held them for as long as she could. The Captain needs to go first if you don't have any other questions. Connecting to his energy before felt bad, but having his energy in front of me is awful. Whatever he did to you could have been so much worse. I am in no way diminishing what happened to you, but he was a sick son of a bitch. You have strong guides, angels, and ancestors around you who kept him away. He doesn't like what you are doing, which tells me you are on the right path.

"I think you have done an excellent job with what you have put together. Unfortunately, there are questions you will not ever get answers to. You will suspect things and be accurate almost all the time, but not all of them will be able to be proven with empirical data. I do feel some loose ends that still aren't hidden, and when I say 'hidden,' I mean for good. They are hidden in this world, but they are not gone completely. There's still a chance for one of them. You must be careful about how you approach it.

"I would pull the thread on Jane; she has more information connected to her. She is not happy about this either. We hear about people like this on the news, but when you are directly confronted with this type of evil, it puts things in perspective. These people committed the biggest sin because they murdered innocence. They took the goodness brought through from the other side and forever changed it. It is taking a clean slate and writing the most horrible story you could on it.

"Not everyone is strong like you. I know you have been through your own tough times, but you had a journey to become a phoenix, and you got to where you had to be over time. And while these demons walk the earth, I think angels like you are sent here to ring the bell and let people know they are not alone and that it is unacceptable . . . fight back."

Gerard listened for a moment. "Your mother loves you and is so proud of you. She worries about you, not so much that you are in danger but that the peace which should be in your mind and in your heart at times is not. She understands why, but she still hopes you find peace soon. She knows that you still have work to do. There's more to be found, and that house is your focus. It is poetically the beginning and the end. It is where this all started, and it is where this journey ends. Don't push too fast. If you move too quickly, you'll miss certain things, on a cerebral level and on a spiritual level too."

Gerard took a deep breath and closed his eyes. "Why do I keep seeing a clock and hearing a bell toll? I think I'm getting pulled to a memory in the house. I wouldn't be surprised if a memory comes back to you of hearing a clock chime. During your next time with Jaime, find a grandfather clock with a heavy chime sound to pull the memory. This is key, but I recommend doing it with her so she can balance your energy as memories surface. She will have to prepare. She will know what to do. It is a clue that spirit is passing on for you to use to access a hidden memory."

Gerard was enveloped in a strong smell of roses and asked what my connection was to the name Rose.

"It is connected to my grandmother."

He said, "She is around you a lot. She is the backbone spiritually for you." Gerard smiled. "She said your mother is helping you, but she is leading you and putting you where you need to be." Gerard laughed and said, "I like her. She says she is doing it the way you need it to be done, not the way you want it done. She knows you get frustrated with certain things you can't find or put together, but this is the way it must be done. I say, 'Trust her.' She has a beautiful, pure soul. It's refreshing to have her here."

I spoke with complete and honest bewilderment. "I cannot understand how this went on for so long and no one stepped up and did anything about it."

Gerard said, "Your grandmother said, 'There were the glory days of this. It went on for a period, then collapsed and shut down.'

"The group broke apart. For a time, this ran like a well-oiled machine. Something connected to you occurred and brought it toward collapse. After, instead of acting as a group, they went their separate ways. You will learn this information eventually. There were some twisted people surrounded by many fearful, scared people, and, combined, they all allowed it to get to where it did. Because of the networks of who knew who, the connections to the underworld, real or not, the people who knew and felt complicit because they did not do anything to stop it, this went on for quite some time. Also, the questionable deaths of two people that occurred in the community who may have threatened to speak up made many good people look the other way."

Gerard continued: "You have homework to do. You are on the right path. I want you to be careful with the timing of things. I think you need to push forward, but you must find the right pace and rhythm. From what spirit conveys and from what you've told me, Jaime and your work with her is a godsend for you. She is doing all the right things. I think she is keeping you level, energy-wise. I think without her this would be a dark journey for you, even darker than what it is." He quieted for a moment and then said, "This is a reminder from spirit. Find a grandfather clock chime sound to help pull the memory. Do it in a safe space with Jaime, where she can help you through it. We should meet again afterward. This is the point you need to get to before spirit can reveal more."

After the session, I organized and cataloged the information I'd received. I was brought back to Mother's confession. There were many people she did not protect me from. Her confession only revealed a sliver of the entire truth, but it was enough to prompt this investigation. Whoever The Old Man was, and the house he lived in, would be the next, and what seemed like the last, clue I needed to complete this puzzle. I drew a large question mark next to "Old Man" and traced my pen back and forth along the line connecting him to The Captain's box on the hierarchy chart. I was more determined than ever to keep digging until I uncovered the complete truth.

The next morning, not following Gerard's recommendations, I found a grandfather clock chime sound and sat quietly in a meditative state and listened. I sank in quickly as the sound penetrated my entire being. It did not just enter my ears; it entered every cell in my body. My skin felt like there were thousands of bugs crawling on it. I felt nauseous and scared. Overcome, I stopped the sound. My heart raced. I panicked and regretted my decision to do it alone. I was not sure if I could revisit this.

A few days later, I had a startling vision dream. I was in an apartment in my childhood neighborhood. It was the house Gerard and I had spoken about. There was an orgy taking place. I could not see in detail, but I could perceive shadowy figures moving slowly in a darkened room. There were other smaller figures present, other children. I could see myself in the middle of what looked like a sea of shadows, tossing and churning. I was small; my eyes were giant and lit up like a photograph was being taken, the flash reflecting in my wide-eyed gaze. My hair on one side was sticking straight out, and something was on the side of my face.

A woman entered the room and screamed, "There are children here!"

A man leaning on a stool grabbed her and said, "Don't worry about it."

They could not calm her down; she was frantic. In the confusion, I made my way outside. There were people on the porch.

It was 1:04 a.m. Someone said the police were coming. I started walking, but I was an adult and the time changed to 6:38 a.m. I pulled out my cell phone and called Alex. In a whisper, I asked him to come and rescue me before they found me.

I woke shaking and in a disturbed state. I knew I was being given information from spirit, details of the truth surrounding the person Gerard mentioned, The Old Man, who was the leader of this group and connected to the house where everything started. The House of Secrets.

Weeks later, I dreamed of the house again. The location was clearer this time. I was back in the apartment with several young people, none of whose faces I could recognize. I was in a small child's body again. Suddenly, everyone became startled, scared, and moved around the room looking for a place to hide. Someone was coming, and this person was dangerous. The name was spoken, but I could not hear it. I was outside on the sidewalk. It was 6:00 a.m. and I had to walk home. On the way, I stopped at St. Paul's schoolyard. I walked in and saw small children standing with parents, waiting for the school to open. As I walked toward the exit, a large bear- or wolflike creature attacked me from behind. I felt its teeth scraping against the back of my head, its saliva dripping down my back, and its hot breath on my neck. It hopped off when a family appeared and called out to it. I was awakened by a soft bark and breath on my face. When I opened my eyes, I expected to see my dog standing there, but she was fast asleep on her bed on the floor.

My already-intense investigation ramped up even further, and I continued my research by looking through the property records of the houses on the street I knew was referenced in my vision dream. Combining the owner information with census lists from Ancestry, I was able to find exactly what I was looking for. It was like a brick dropped on my head. The House of Secrets was where Jane had grown up. Gerard had mentioned that pulling the string on her would lead to more information. It all came together. Through census and court records, I learned her parents had divorced when she was young, and she and her mother moved in with her grandparents. The Old Man, who had been like a father figure to The Captain, was her grandfather. He had other children, one a junior with the same name. It was her family who was the connection.

My next session with Gerard was not for another three months. I reminded myself I needed to be patient and allow the process to flow as it had been. It had been six years since I first lifted the seal on my secrets. It was hard to control my eagerness to move forward now that I was getting so close to knowing the whole truth. I went inward over the next few weeks, a perfect time to do so during the coldest period of the Vermont winter. I concentrated on my studies in energy medicine. This was what kept me focused and grounded throughout my journey. Without it, I do not know how I would have navigated the methodical, painstaking discovery of such surreal and life-changing imagery and disclosures.

Throughout this journey, I spent countless hours researching the people involved in this story to be sure I was piecing together the details correctly and that all was consistent with the information I was receiving in vision dreams, from my work with Gerard, and from each of my helpers. Some of the details of this story had to be methodically searched for and carefully pieced together, but others appeared with little effort. It all merged into a flow that remained fluid throughout this story.

My efforts continued to uncover secrets. Surprisingly, I was matched to another half sibling through Ancestry. He had been born in 1955. I reached out, and after several messages, it was revealed he was from Father.

After returning from the Korean War, Father had been stationed in New Mexico and had a relationship with a woman that produced a child. He returned to Staten Island in late summer the same year and never had any further contact with them.

My parents were stunningly flawed individuals who left behind a trail of children, individually and together, fated to carry the consequences of their abundantly poor choices and burdened with the same hereditary lack of emotional support and generational trauma they also faced. *Will there be more?*

It is the children of parents who endured difficult childhoods and were saddled with unresolved trauma who bear the weight of unspoken family secrets. Parents pass on not only their eye color or certain personality traits but also their own experiences of trauma to the next generation. This creates dysfunctional emotional damage, which has a real impact on the health and happiness of the often-fractured family unit. It ripples out through communities to the greater human spirit.

My parents could not offer more as caretakers than their limited developmental allowance knew and instead passed on the same unconscious results of creating deep resentment and broken parent-child bonds.

Until someone breaks the cycle, these toxic behaviors can endure from generation to generation. Genes influence but do not permanently determine our personality traits. We are in control. We have free will.

Chapter Fifteen

THE SUN, THE MOON, AND THE TRUTH

Ninety days later, Gerard and I met for our next session, but, unfortunately, things did not go as planned. Gerard explained how while meditating before our call, he had felt a lump in his throat. This had happened in our previous session, but we still connected. This time, we did not advance. Spirit conveyed a message that I needed to be aware of an important detail first. I needed this information before we could move forward. A crucial piece of the puzzle was missing. It was the last and most important piece.

The night before this session with Gerard, I had been given the information I needed through a vision dream, but I was not able to piece it together in time. It was another disturbing dream from which I woke trembling and in distress. I had dreamed I was floating in water. I was in my small-child body. In the next moment, I stood with a woman, clutching her waist with all my strength. A man and woman walked toward me. They were going to take me. I was terrified. I knew they were going to hurt me. In an instant, I was underwater, struggling to get to the surface. I felt the sensation of not being able to breathe. I heard myself scream and saw the bubbles rising in front of my face. I woke myself out of this horrible vision. I was sweating and my heart was racing. As I lay there, I felt a presence and heard my name spoken clearly.

At the time, I had been reading about past lives and reincarnation and assumed this vision dream offered images of how I had died in a past life. In my journal, I wrote the date and, underneath, "Glimpse into a Past Life" and a brief description. The night of the suspended session with Gerard, before going to sleep, I asked spirit to help me understand what I was missing to move forward.

The following morning, I wrote, "They tried to kill me! Someone threw me in water! The woman I was holding on to was Mother. They tried to make it look like an accident. A drowning!" I had been thrown into our backyard swimming pool. The pool had been torn down shortly after this, so it would not be attempted again. They wanted to shut me up.

I raced through my journal to review my notes and sessions to look for the word "water." The entire time, I repeated, "Please let me be wrong this time, please let me be wrong this time." Water was referenced several times, but one stood out. The familiar flow of energy ran through my body, indicating I was on the right track. Father had even given the name of the person who did it.

In the notes from my sixth session with Celine, I had written, "She (Mother) is showing three steps on the side of a house. There is a clothesline, a large tree, and water. There is significance to the water. He (Father) is repeating a name, Silvio . . . he was threatened by him with a knife. He thought he would be murdered or hurt. After inquiring about who The Captain was and if I was given to him for money, Celine had replied, 'Yes. I keep getting something about water. They keep referencing water.'"

I also found the words my grandmother had spoken during my third session with Gerard. "Something connected to you occurred and brought it toward collapse. Instead of doing this as a group, they went their separate ways. You will learn this information eventually." This was the connection.

It was over two weeks until my next meeting with Gerard, and now I had the information I needed to move forward . . . I'd had it all along. Emotionally, coming to this realization was even more debilitating than Mother's confession, which I did not think was possible. This detail was an important piece in completing this shocking and sickening puzzle.

While investigating the name Silvio and concentrating on the happenings of that day, I had a lot of questions. What had happened to bring something of this magnitude about? Someone obviously took me out of the water, but who? I believe this happened during the summer of 1975. I was four years old. Had I started to talk about what was happening? I would not have been the first person they had gotten rid of to protect themselves. Now I knew why I was so afraid of water. Mother had told me as a child that I became afraid of water after seeing the movie *Jaws*. I have no memory of seeing the movie until well into adulthood, but I do remember the pool being taken down.

It was strange what memories became clear after new doors into this story were opened. I recalled a hose was put into the pool, with the other end tucked under the fence and into the gutter, which filled with water until the pool was empty. I sat on the front steps of our apartment building and watched the water float down to the end of the street.

Here I was again, plunged into my continuing education on how to tolerate the intolerable and accept the unacceptable. How did I survive this? How would I survive knowing this?

I held close the words of my grandmother: "It has been in the blood for generations, molestation and abuse. I was a victim too. You broke the cycle by speaking the truth. The ones who push back at you are not the ones you need. There has been enough silence. You are the voice of all the victims, and the light you shine will become a beacon after the storm."

I braced myself for my next conversation with Gerard. *Please let me be wrong.*

While waiting for Gerard to join our session, a crushing sense of dread washed over me as I needed to confirm the details of what I knew and learn more about what I did not. I was also excited to be so near to completing my investigation after all these years of intense and emotionally hard work. Besides the usual attendees, I also called in The Perpetrators and anyone else who was willing to provide details. Gerard joined the video call and mentioned that he felt heavy words would be spoken today. I agreed, and instead of our usual friendly chat, we began immediately.

Gerard called in spirit and read the roll call. "Your mom showed up during our introductions. She came through immediately. Your aunt and other members of your father's family are here. They say you did not know them in life, but they are here as support or to speak on matters the others may not divulge."

Gerard did not know I had called in The Perpetrators.

"I have The Priest, The Captain, and The Old Man we spoke about last time. The Old Man was the leader, the one The Captain idolized, the one who lived in The House of Secrets. It was more than a mentorship; The Old Man was telling him what to do, giving orders. He is the one connected to the clock."

Gerard closed his eyes. "I keep seeing that clock. It's right next to him; he liked to tinker with it. Throughout our sessions, we have had a cast of characters who do not reside in the light, but The Old Man was the most deceptive in his physical appearance. He looks like a sweet old man, a tinkerer, quiet, yet he is a horrible, horrible individual. When I connect to them, I feel a hierarchy here. Are you asking if you met him as a child?"

I said, "Yes, I know I have."

Gerard continued, "It's almost like you were paraded in front of . . . ." Gerard struggled with his words, and with sorrow in his voice he said, "The way farmers show prized animals. That is the way it comes across. Children were brought to him. You were not the only one. He was the brains behind the operation. They all operated individually but were still woven together to some degree. He is at the top. Your mom said, 'The buck stops here.'

Gerard asked aloud, "What is the significance of the clock? Why do I keep seeing it?"

Then he said, "He lived and died by that clock. Everything was timed out and measured, controlled and predictable. He used the chime of the clock to time out meetings and sessions. It was his marker for how fast or slow he had to move."

I asked, "Does it still exist?"

"Yes, but it has been sold and moved around. It holds negative energy. I am pulled west. It goes from one owner to the next. The Old Man has the feel of an earthbound spirit and is likely still connected to it."

After a moment of quiet, he continued, "The Old Man molested boys and girls but mostly girls. Your mom added, 'He was the broker. He arranged things and tried them out beforehand. It was about purity. He had to get before anyone else.'

"We have had evil people come through with this story, but he is by far the worst."

To summarize, I said to Gerard, "Jane, who married, Giovanni, was one of the three perpetrators below The Captain. Giovanni and The Business Man were the other two. The Old Man was her grandfather. He had a son named Junior. Theirs was The House of Secrets."

Gerard said in disgust, "The Old Man said, 'I found my heir to the throne.' My mind went right to Junior, but he shook his head no, and your mom pulled me to The Old Man's daughter, Jane's mother, to show the connection. Jane was the heir to the throne."

He continued, "Jane was ruthless, and when I say 'ruthless,' I am not only talking about the molestation. She liked controlling people and putting them in bad positions. Not to diminish the others who were driven by sick impulses, but she was calculating. She has not evolved. If she had another lifetime, I could see her wanting to hurt people. She gets joy from it. She is stepping out from behind, and I know she thinks she said something matter-of-fact, but it's sickening the way she said it.

"She said, 'It was a business to me; I was making money.' To her, she didn't care who she hurt; she didn't even think about it. She held no loyalty to anyone. When I am pulled to her mothering energy, she is like a "mommy dearest" and held a veneer of being a stereotypical mom. It all started with the history of this one family. The evil seeds were planted there. As horrible as The Old Man feels, his granddaughter, Jane, is somehow even worse. Sometimes she had a hard time keeping up appearances, it slipped occasionally, and she showed her fierce anger."

Gerard continued, "Junior was also involved. He worked through people's emotions. He had a big ego and thought highly of himself. He also had a bad temper. He liked to squeeze people's arms and jerk them around. It was all about control." Then he asked, "Do you have memories of this place?"

I responded, "When I found the house in the property-search records and connected the details, I had clear memories of being there. The way the front of the house looked, the second-floor windows in particular, the porch. It was not a single-family house. It was two apartments. My vision dreams about being there helped my repressed memories become clearer. They are difficult, excruciating memories. The night before our previous meeting, I was given the key piece of information that was needed to move further, but I didn't connect it until the following morning."

Gerard said, "Your mom is saying, 'The Old Man is the end of the line. All things begin and end with him. Once he is put into place, it starts becoming your story, not theirs. You focus so much on the cast of characters and the events, but now, from this point on, you will start focusing on you, what you have been through, how you have processed it, how you are feeling, and how you have managed to heal the scars you have from it.'"

Gerard asked me, "Do you have any questions?"

I replied, "Yes. For the last few months, I have been getting visions and information from spirit to gradually uncover my memories of what happened in The Old Man's house. This is hard to say, but I know that I, along with a few other children, were present during an orgy happening there."

Gerard said, "I am seeing four kids total. The Old Man oversaw everything. I'm hearing that soon after this night, something happened that made them dismantle the group. I see two kids looking at each other. I keep feeling, 'Who's going to help us?'"

Gerard asked, "Do you remember a little boy there? I feel one boy, the rest were girls, including you. Your mom brings me to you, thinking, *Who is going to save us, and when is this going to stop?* This is horrible. They were like a pack of animals."

I took deep breaths and responded, "As you mentioned, I think something happened after this night that may have disrupted their plans going forward."

Gerard replied, "Your mother is saying, 'That was the night things started to change.'"

I continued, "In my vision, a woman came through the door, saw what was happening, and screamed at the top of her lungs, 'There are kids here!'"

Gerard said, "She was the wife of one of the men in the group. It was more than screaming; it was complete horror and panic. One person was trying to shush her."

I responded, "That was in my vision. A man who was leaning on a stool grabbed her and said, 'Don't worry about it.'"

Gerard said, "It took threats to shut her up. She was beaten."

I asked, "Will they say who it was? I'm feeling it is The Business Man."

Gerard said, "I am being pulled to the bar."

I responded, "Yes, that's him."

Validated, he continued, "He's the connection; it was his wife. That was the night they realized they couldn't keep getting together in a group. It drew too much attention. They realized they had to lay low."

I said, "I think someone called the police."

Gerard said, "She did. The wife of The Business Man. That's why she got a beating, but I don't think the police ever made it to the house. It was squashed. The group came to an agreement that there could not be more than two of them together at the same time."

In a quiet, pained voice, I said, "I think I was four years old."

Gerard agreed and held up his writing pad showing the number four written several times. "This night didn't stop things, but it did change things. When I am pulled to The Business Man, it worked out for him in a way. He wasn't under the watchful eye of The Old Man as he was before, so he took liberties to do his own stuff afterward, without the group. It loosened the reins. Everything during this time revolved around this core group of kids. Others were in and out at times, but this was the core group who were brought back from time to time."

Gerard said, "They are paying for it on the other side. The only reason they are here right now is because they are allowed to be. The Perpetrators are not good, and they have zero interest in atoning. From the time you started until now, the only one who developed any remorse is The Priest. None for the others. They are the same as they were when they lived. What you have opened and forced acknowledgment of has given them all a chance to evolve, but The Priest is the only one advancing. He still has a long way to go to be anywhere good. The others do not want any help."

I said, "I believe this group is tied to what happened to me at St. Paul's. There were a few priests and at least one nun who knew what was happening."

Gerard said, "When I see the vestments, I see the ranks of order, each involved at a different level. One priest who comes through says, 'I didn't touch but I didn't speak up.'

"It's the sin of knowing and keeping quiet. The others didn't know. One suspected and mentioned something but was dismissed because he was always classified as a discontented person and a troublemaker. They stopped listening to him, truth or not."

I was about to turn the conversation toward my vision dream of the water when Gerard's computer muted. This had happened before in previous sessions when sensitive information was about to be communicated. Gerard said someone did not want this part of the story to be told. It went further this time, and my computer completely lost power.

After reconnecting, I said, "I think something happened shortly after that night at The House of Secrets, where someone tried to hurt me in a different way, other than the molestation."

Gerard's computer muted again. The lamp behind him dimmed several times. I wished we had not chosen a nighttime session. For the first time throughout this process, I felt scared, yet I took it as further validation and continued, "I think I was getting older, my vocabulary more advanced, and they were worried I might talk."

Gerard asked, "Do you remember people altering your memory, telling you it did not happen?"

"Yes, mostly my mother. She continued that manipulation throughout my life."

Gerard said, "For her, it was a combination of not being found out and remorse of wanting you to forget. The mentality of, 'If you don't speak about it, it doesn't exist.' She thought it would fade away with time. She did not understand the psychology. In a sense, it was one of the few protective things she did, although it was too little too late, and the damage was done. It's like shooting someone in the stomach, apologizing, and putting a Band-Aid on it. Her intent was a couple of things: fear of being caught; understanding the gravity of it; feeling bad she allowed it to happen; and hoping you would forget. They believed you were young enough to not remember."

I replied, "I did not remember any details of abuse besides what happened to me with The Teenager and The Priests when I started this work. Although I always intuitively knew something terrible happened to me when I was young. I feel like I am watching a movie about someone else's life."

Gerard said, "The memories are encoded in your hard drive. They are unraveling now naturally, as you explore them with the help of spirit. Remember, there are three things you can't hide: the sun, the moon, and the truth. It's the truest expression ever. You can try to avoid it, ignore it, suppress it, but it cannot be hidden forever."

I deeply understood now how everything Mother told me was a lie used to manipulate and confuse my memories. These years of putting together this puzzle had been the assembling of the truth.

Although these words were unspoken, Gerard agreed, "Yes, and for varying reasons, some to hurt, some to protect, some to move on. There are many gray areas when we come to your immediate family, while the others are black-and-white. With your family, except for a few, there is an understanding that mistakes were made. They were being forced into certain things. They felt they could be killed if they spoke up. There were regrets. I don't feel the sickness of it as I do with the others. There are different motivations here, all horrible."

Throughout the session, I had been preparing to ask about the water and how they tried to kill me. I finally blurted it out: "Will someone speak up about how they tried to silence me?"

Gerard asked, "Do you have a recollection of being physically harmed, aside from the molestation?"

I replied, "Yes, I do."

He added, "Your mom is bringing up how you were beaten as an intimidation tactic. They tried to put fear into you to make sure you never spoke up. It was physical, not just verbal. She is deeply sorry for this. She has evolved on the other side; she is quite different from who she was in the physical. Your parents were flawed people who did horrible things. The regret is there now, but in the moment, they were controlled by fear more than anything and by people around them. They felt like they were backed into a corner, and they worried about your voice hurting them and the family, not just legally but physically. These were not good people around them."

I was utterly disgusted. They were cowards, all of them, and they failed not only me but also the other children who were abused. I gathered the courage to say, "I think they tried to kill me and make it look like an accident."

At the same time, speaking over each other and having to repeat ourselves in turn to understand, Gerard repeated how he felt like I was brought to the brink of death and asked, "What is the water connection with you?"

I gasped. After a few seconds, I continued, "Following our last session, when they would not speak because I was missing an important piece of the puzzle, I recalled a vision dream I'd had the night before. I was floating on water in my small child-hood body. I assumed I was dead. Next, I was clutching the waist of a woman. I believe it was my mother. A man and a woman were walking toward me; they were going to take me. I knew they were going to hurt me. I was scared and crying. Then I was submerged, sinking, drowning in water. I screamed and bubbles came out of my mouth and rose in front of my face. I interpreted it as a glimpse into a past life, and I did not connect the dots in time. The day after our session when I woke, it hit me. Someone tried to kill me by throwing me in the pool in our backyard. They tried to drown me and make it look like it was an accident." My body filled with the telltale energy vibration of truth. I felt a soft, warm hand resting on my left shoulder.

Gerard said, "Yes, you are correct. I see it is a perfect sunny day." He shook his head, the sadness on his face visible as he scribbled on his pad.

Gerard cleared his throat. "A male was brought in as someone connected to the group who was going to take care of it. Your mother knew what was going on. I'm so sorry to say this, but she was going to let it happen. She went into the apartment with the male's wife. She couldn't watch or hear what was happening, and after you were thrown in, she immediately ran back outside and took you out of the pool."

Surprised, I asked, "She was the one who took me out of the water?"

Gerard said, "Yes."

I added, "The pool was taken down around this time. Was this the reason?"

He said, "Yes. They made up a bunch of excuses as to why, but the only reason was so it was not attempted again."

I asked, "So it was directed by the group for someone to kill me by throwing me in the water and making it look like I accidentally drowned? The man and woman in my dream who were coming to take me . . . I know it was them."

Gerard replied, "The woman took your mother inside the apartment. The man was there to do the deed; she was there to disarm."

I asked, "Was I taken to the hospital?"

"No, I don't think you were in the water long enough. After it happened, your mother's instant regret, worry, and motherly instinct kicked in, and she didn't think about any repercussions; she jumped in and took you out."

I wondered how I survived all of this. I was brought close to death several times—at the hands of others, and sadly at my own hands later. Much like I allowed anger and rage to flow through me during the uncovering of this story, I let complete misery and sadness do the same.

I took a moment to gather my thoughts and said, "Well, it was the first and only time she had a motherly instinct."

Gerard agreed. "It's why I used the word 'instinct.' It kicked in after hearing the splash. She didn't think about it; a momentary impulse took her over."

I asked, "Did anyone else know?"

Gerard said, "No, this was the biggest hush-hush. When your mother pulled me to the water, I felt the water flush over your head and your face. I felt your panic."

I could not form the words I wanted to say: *They fucking tried to kill me! How much crazier can this story get?*

Gerard explained this event was the pinnacle of it.

"What about the other kids?"

Gerard said, "They were more controllable, more pliable. I feel fear, sadness, and depression, pulling inward and quieting. You were different, the opposite. You wouldn't stop asking questions and talking about what was going on. You wouldn't let it go. They knew you were a mistake after a while. They knew you had a fighter spirit. You were already the type of child who questioned everything, but they didn't expect this type of behavior from you. You have a fight, a stubbornness in you.

"This will always be a part of you. You can't let this go completely; it is what shaped you into who you are. You have taken it in a productive and healing direction and will help other people, but it's still part of who you are, good, bad, or indifferent. This is heavy. Molestation is a heavy topic, but to the degree this went is crazy."

I asked if things stopped after this for me.

"Yes. The fractures in the group started with The Business Man's wife walking in and what happened to you afterward. You inadvertently stopped the ring from operating together. You managed to start the takedown of the unit by merely being yourself. They went on separately, but it did diminish and instilled a fear factor.

"They operated for a long time, thinking they couldn't be touched, but it slowly started crumbling, partly from their own sloppiness and partly because of you. Our souls retain characteristics, whether on this side or the other. We come in with a certain personality type, and our experiences either enhance or diminish it, but at the core we maintain who we are. You had a fight in you as a child, not as fierce as it is now, but the spark was there."

After a pause, Gerard said, "Your mom said that's enough for today."

I agreed.

Gerard added, "This process has not only helped you; it has also helped your mom. I think about how she's evolved from the first time I connected with her to now. She has tried all along to bring healing to you. It was why she was so forthcoming with information and why she timed it as she did. There were times she gave it all and times she knew you weren't ready. This was a journey of the soul for her too. Her energy feels vastly different. She's immensely proud of you and what you are doing. She loves you and she worries about you. This is a purging that needed to happen to bring you to the next stage of your journey. This stage was about you. The next stage is about others . . . for you to bring healing to others, and not only with the book."

Elated to hear these words, I thought of how I felt when I was writing. Like I was doing what I was supposed to be doing for the first time.

Gerard continued, "Your mother loves you and is sorry for what has happened. Acknowledge your pain and understand where it comes from, but don't let it become a security blanket. Your mom was spectacularly imperfect, but she was a victim too. It doesn't take away from the anger, but it will help you heal. It's a lot to unpack. The other side knows better than we do; their timing on giving information was for a reason."

"I'm sorry, I must backtrack here a bit. When I was taken to the water connection, the way the image flooded in, it took me by surprise. I did not expect it. Even after everything we talked about, I didn't see it coming, which is rare. Your parents guided this part of the story carefully. Remember, you first received a signal of something of great importance happening around water almost three years ago. They wanted you to know this crucial and final piece of the puzzle but in small clues and stages. It is quite shocking."

I said, "I did not see it coming either. When it did, I immediately categorized it as a past-life image. This is exceptionally hard to navigate emotionally. It is numbingly painful to know that my mother knew what they were going to do to me and planned to let it happen."

Gerard concluded with, "We come into the physical with a soul contract. This is yours or part of it. You are throwing a large rock into a small pond, causing ripples. It is necessary to throw the rock; sometimes things need to be shaken up. Change rarely, if ever, comes without a tumultuous event. This is life-changing not only for you but also for many people, if you stay true to your voice."

I thanked Gerard for walking on this road with me and mentioned how I was sure it had not been easy for him, considering the subject matter. I wondered if these were the most intense sessions he had ever had.

We had a good laugh, and he said, "Other people ask about their marriage, their job, etc. You have bigger fish to fry."

Chapter Sixteen

THE DEVIL IS
IN THE DETAILS

The expression "The devil is in the details" derives from the phrase "God is in the details."

This earlier version originated in the 1800s and had a different connotation than the modern phrasing. The idea was that whatever one does should be done thoroughly, and the truth, if it exists, is in the details.

Even minute details can have a significant impact. Details can be hidden aspects of this world. They are not always apparent and may even seem insignificant, but they are always present and point to understanding the essence of a situation. The remembrance of one small detail can lead to a larger recollection repeatedly, until the whole picture emerges.

I understood clearly there were many devils in the details I had uncovered.

As I reached the end of my story, secure in knowing I had all the information I needed to reclaim myself fully, I met with Wendy for a final soul-retrieval session. I explained the new details, including the information about the back seat of the car, The

House of Secrets, and the shocking attempt made to end my life by throwing me into the pool. Wendy and my other helpers had learned of my story alongside me in increments and stood with me through each step. They each supported my healing process and helped me regain what was stolen. They provided the guidance I needed to help me navigate this journey.

After the familiar soothing ritual of sage and sounds, Wendy connected with the whale shaman. The first stop was the back seat of the car. The initial impression she sensed was of being held down with a hand over her mouth, squirming and trying to break loose. She described the car as a large 1970s model with a bench seat, four doors, and a vinyl top. The surrounding area had dirt everywhere, and something was above the car, like an overpass. There were construction materials around, and she smelled burning in the air, like sulfur or an industrial type of odor.

My mind raced back to the conversation with Gerard, who mentioned the smell of sulfur when we spoke about this.

Wendy perceived how my soul piece had left the car and gone to another part of the construction site, where she sat on a mound of stones and was surrounded by many pigeons. Wendy observed the tiny girl picking up small stones and throwing them to the pigeons to see if they would try to eat them. One pigeon stood out. It was not acting as part of the group but stood at the outer edge staring at her. Wendy and the whale shaman connected with her and introduced themselves. They told her they would take her to her grown-up home where she would be safe. She immediately stood and was willing to join them, but she did not want to leave the one pigeon behind. She bent to carefully pick it up, gently held it in her arms, and took it along with them.

Pigeons have an extraordinary homing sense and know how to find their way back home no matter how far they have gone. Pigeon represented my true essence, my lost and dissociated soul parts, which are now restored and welcomed back home to a pure and loving space.

Wendy and the whale shaman moved on to The House of Secrets. The first impression was of unpleasant scents. The lighting was dim, and Wendy saw a flash of light. It was the flash of a camera.

My soul part was trapped in a photograph. When the photo was taken, the soul part went into the flash of light and became trapped in the film. Wendy and the whale shaman retrieved it out of the image.

I was drawn to my vision dream of what happened to me in The House of Secrets. When I saw my eyes, they were enormous and brightly lit in a darkened room. I perceived how they reflected the flash of a camera and seemed frozen in that moment of time.

Next was the backyard. Wendy heard frantic splashing and had a strong sensory overload of the smell of chlorine and the feeling of choking underwater. She felt panic. Everything was happening fast. She heard screaming under the water. She saw the bubbles rising. My soul part left as soon as I knew danger was coming, before I was even thrown into the pool. Wendy and the whale shaman found me sitting on the other side of the wall that separated the pool from the front sidewalk. I sat against the wall with my knees to my chest, covering my ears and looking across the street at a tree. Another aspect of me was lost besides the soul part; it was my voice. My young voice had an inner power and was strong, but after this, it was quieted. This was not the voice I found when I first spoke my truth, not my fighting voice; this was my pure voice. It was abstract. My voice was symbolized by a chickadee perched in the tree I was focused on. As Wendy and the whale shaman approached, I retrieved the chickadee and melted into the whale shaman with no resistance.

Wendy and her allies and helpers worked to integrate the retrieved parts into harmony within me. She reminded me to use photographs of myself during the time periods associated with the soul-retrieval work we had done as an integration tool, to look directly into my eyes and welcome that part of myself back into my body, with the assurance that it was safe to do so now.

When I arrived home, I dug into the back of my small file cabinet until my fingers found the bright-purple folder with the word "photos" written on the tab. I was ready to do this work.

I spent time looking directly into my eyes in each of the photographs, assuring my younger self that we have a happy and peaceful life now and that it is safe for her to come home. I told her she created a beautiful life for herself. I told her she is like a lotus flower who had learned to hold the wisdom of her life without the stains of the murky and muddy waters from which she came.

In *The Body Keeps the Score*, trauma is defined as unbearable and intolerable.[13] You will do anything to not think about the events leading to the trauma or even acknowledge the terrible happenings themselves by developing a forced forgetting. It is a deeply embedded survival strategy. Except you are not forgetting. You are pushing the memories into your body at a cellular level, where they will live and eventually surface. Large amounts of energy are needed to keep them suppressed. Holding memories of "terror" in denial does not make them go away, and they tend to surface when you least expect it.

Trauma lives forever within and rears its ugly head sometimes unexpectedly, as well as on anticipated occasions when you can attempt to brace yourself for impact. During the 2018 Senate Judiciary Committee hearing on Supreme Court nominee Brett Kavanaugh, the most powerful moment of Dr. Christine Blasey Ford's testimony came when Vermont senator Patrick Leahy asked her to describe her strongest memory from the night of the alleged assault.

Dr. Ford responded, "The laughter. Indelible in the hippocampus is the laughter."[14]

I was braced for impact with the subject at hand but still deeply touched by her statement because what I remembered most from the molestation I endured from my teenage neighbor as a young girl was the laughter from him and his friends when they first entered my apartment. Laughter was supposed to convey happiness, but in this case, it conveyed terror and became etched in my brain as a warning of potential danger.

As I grew into adulthood, I was able to put this scene into context, but those memories would always enter. This experience also left me with a lifelong need to have doors and windows locked.

An unlocked door brings me right to the sensation of being in danger. The understanding of why this feeling of being unsafe still holds influence over me and the actions I take to remedy it is an important part of healing. Within reason, it is important to do what it takes to feel safe.

Dr. Ford's mention of the hippocampus led me to further explore and understand how the brain of a child impacted by sexual abuse functions under stress and how the adult version of the child is shaped by these experiences. In coordination with reading many books and research studies, podcasts, and any other form of information I could learn from, I understood why what happened to me resulted in so much upheaval in each phase of my life. Layers of additional trauma and stress continued because I was not adjusted, relaxed, or able to feel fully safe, and it caused disruption in all areas.

Early life trauma impacts brain function during a time when it is at its most vulnerable state and is a major risk factor in developing psychological problems, suicidality, anxiety, and addiction. In children, there is already a limited amount of self-control due to the underdeveloped prefrontal cortex. Understanding this and how my hard-to-control impulses were caused by actual changes in brain function, not a lack of moral character or being a flawed or bad person, was key to mending the stigmas I lived with. I was easily drawn into believing this as a young person. It had been used as a tool to keep me quiet. Learning and understanding these facts were a key part to healing. It helped lift the blanket of shame and the loss of self-worth that caused these feelings and kept them alive into adulthood.

The hippocampus is highly affected by stress and is the area of the brain that helps form our memory function. It is informed by the amygdala, the alarm section of the brain, to remember things that are unsafe and related to danger. The amygdala detects threats, and the resulting emotional intensity assigns the famous fight-or-flight-or-freeze response.

The thalamus is the mail sorter of the brain, sending sensory information to different areas and alerting the subconscious when safety is threatened. These alerts can be through smell, sound, or other physical or emotional sensations. The hypothalamus, the area of the brain that controls unconscious functions and maintains the homeostasis of the body, such as regulating temperature, hunger, and reactions to stress, can become disrupted by trauma and can lead to emotional and physical health issues. The hypothalamus uses hormones that lead the reaction to the alarm or threat. Trauma alters these neural responses. Understanding brain function helped me understand why I rarely feel completely safe and initially interpret many situations as potential threats that I must quickly discern.

More importantly, I learned how it is possible to reverse these changes and rewire sections of the brain.

Many survivors of sexual assault cannot bear to remember. It takes a considerable amount of work to find the strength to get past the agonizing shame and allow yourself to access the memories. Instead, we avoid and misdirect ourselves from the truth and turn to and live in an alternate reality. Lying can be done through complete silence as well as made-up stories.

I regularly lied about my childhood and home life, my relationship with Mother, and my past overall, doing my best to appear "normal." I created stories to fit this narrative. My childhood was not even close to normal, and hiding behind this facade only served to keep me from fully becoming the person I was truly meant to be. Gross distortions and misrepresentations of fact became like living in a parallel universe. Sometimes we must step into the darkness to be able to see a glimpse of light.

Life is a journey of lessons, and we all have a road we need to travel on to learn them. It is a choice to live with secrets and in dimness or to search for the light and live in the truth.

Chapter Seventeen

EMERGENCE

In *The Marriage of Heaven and Hell*, William Blake mocks the oppressive authority of both church and state, describing "shame as pride's cloak," and he speaks of how men forgot that "all deities reside in the human breast," not in the priesthood.[15]

Blake's writing introduced me to his series of watercolor paintings and a particular one that resonated deeply: *The Great Red Dragon and the Woman Clothed with the Sun*, wherein Blake encompasses the duality between good and evil beautifully. At first, I could only see the hovering, threatening demon floating above the woman with chaos all around. The demon's large coiled tail, which looks as if it could easily wrap itself around her neck and choke her, hangs threateningly in midair. The flapping of its wings has caused a flurry of air that lifts her hair up and around her head.

As time went on and I moved forward on my journey, I saw the painting in a different way. After finally relieving myself of the weightiness of keeping secrets, the focal points of the painting became the light emanating from the center of her chest and her raised arms intent on holding the demon back.

Her head is not bent over, quivering in fear; she returns the demon's menacing glare by staring straight into his eyes. She is a light in the darkness. She is without anger. She is truth. She is justice. She is clothed with the radiance of the sun. She is infinitely more powerful than the demon. She is every woman who stands up in dissent.

Similarly, I now see the light emanating from me. It is bright and strong like the woman clothed with the sun. I am stronger than the demons who hovered above me; I always have been.

When the time came, I was ready for this battle. I found the courage to look my demons in the eyes and learn the truth that would finally set me free of their grasp, a truth that would also set the demons free, if they allowed.

Forgiveness is the single most important action you can take for your own complete physical, emotional, and mental health. When your truth connects to a painful and dark history, seemingly unbearable and unforgivable, forgiveness is also the most difficult task.

While things were done deliberately to hurt me, and although my resulting anger was righteous, disassociating and nurturing a grudge was what tricked me into thinking I was in control of the situation.

Our emotions are so powerful, they can easily overtake the ability to reason. We see this in today's volatile society, whose varied toxic ideologies are based on lies and fraught emotions alone, completely lacking in fact, empathy, or thoughtful reason and soaked in shallow incivility. Anger is an embodied emotion that keeps us inflexibly determined in our condemnation. The inability to acknowledge my truth and release my anger is what kept me locked in the past. Authentic forgiveness is not a quick or simple task. Time is needed to do the work necessary to heal. It is part of the journey that unfolds as we process trauma.

There are only two emotions: fear and love. All others stem from these. Today, I choose love over fear. I still struggle with a constant feeling of being unsafe, but I now have a toolbox of remedies and an acceptance of the underlying reasons and root causes.

True freedom came when I realized I had always been free to reclaim my power. It was my choice whether I found the courage to speak my truth or stay small and quiet, protecting the abusers instead of myself. It took decades. I found forgiveness, not for the abusers' crimes against me but for myself, so as to not carry hate in my heart.

There are often ties to unfinished business energetically with others wherein these attributes can heal by clearing old wounds. Healing creates a connection to the divine and to your higher self and erases subconscious energetic imprints from this life, past lives, and within the grid of ancestral trauma, where the memory of wounds causes turmoil in the present.

I learned to release fear, anger, and pain and to recognize it as egoic propaganda. These negative emotions thrived only in my mind, long past the circumstances that created them. I learned that if I could gain a clear awareness of my wounds and stand firmly in my authentic truth, I would carry it for all eternity, long past the point when the body I stand in is gone.

Surrendering to forgiveness is not giving up. Surrendering is going within and finding your power. Discovering your purpose and honoring your authenticity, which has been in your heart since you were born, is a force that leads you to grow, evolve, and learn. We get caught up in the plentiful complexities of life, through outside influence and our own fears, and forget we hold the power to live joyfully, no matter the circumstance. Joy grows out of grace, love, and gratitude. Joy is finding the simple feeling of happiness to be alive. Finding joy is finding freedom.

Stories are everything, and everyone has an important one to tell.

It was through telling my story that I forged my connection

to my heart and soul and found comfort in my own skin. It also allowed me to find and claim my true story and shed the one that was handed down to me.

In writing about my experiences, I gave myself relief from them by externalizing the details. The pain of those details does not live inside me anymore. It still exists, but it is outside of my body. It lives on this paper and in the words themselves. Telling this story has turned me inside out and reshaped me in the most positive way. It allowed me to find true peace in my heart.

The use of various forms of energy medicine served to shine a light on the darkness of my trauma and helped me continue to find my voice. It was the catalyst that propelled me forward and reconfigured my entire life.

Since my initial encounter, I have been studying its effects. The benefit of utilizing energy medicine is to gain the ability to heal yourself and your relationships and find your place of belonging in the world.

I find myself genuinely happy these days. I attract good things into my life and can easily avoid unsavory ones. It is now impossible to resonate with lower frequencies, which serve as an instant repellant. The vibration of higher frequency cannot stop or limit itself, and what does not resonate on the same level will not resonate at all. The clarity of effective healing can be startling at first, as old habits die swiftly, not hard.

I own my story now; it does not own me. It does not hold power over me any longer. It does not lurk in the shadows or creep up from behind when I least expect it. Truth revealed all its hidden secrets. There is nowhere left for them to hide. I am no longer silent, and the feelings of shame and unworthiness no longer hold me in their tight grip. When emotions or memories appear, I hold authority over them. I am in control of the narrative.

Everything has been disclosed, and all the wonders and questions answered, bringing me to where I am today. This story is my remembered and thoroughly investigated version of events and history, and while it can be taken as subjective, I have gone to great lengths to give facts and validate the information. However, due to the nature of the subject, I constantly find myself wishing this story were not real.

I have spent my life wondering why I carried ceaseless heartache. I have answers now. I am conscious of how it was my purpose to bring these injustices to light, and I did not fail in this duty. Reenacting the mistakes of the past by imitating the silence of our ancestors only keeps fractures and wounds alive.

I conclude this story on Independence Day.

My family and I gathered with our community to watch the fireworks on the waterfront. As we waited on the line for creemees, I had a strong and deep knowing how this day was also a celebration of my personal independence. It had been a grueling task, passionately investigating every inch of the past. Both the story and I were now complete. What I truly uncovered was my freedom.

As the fireworks started, the sound of explosions echoing over Lake Champlain resonated through our bodies. We watched as they formed fountains of sparkling colors floating gently above our heads in the shapes of hearts, cascading waterfalls, and smiley faces. We stood close together, huddled under the magnificence of the bursts of color lighting up the sky. I stood squeezed in the middle of the people who I love more than words can express, and who love me back just the same, oohing and aahing in unison.

As we prepared to leave the area after the show, I heard music in the distance, long-familiar lyrics to a song I'd used as a ringtone for the better part of this journey. A reminder that everything will be all right. A message. I am listening.

This life is mine. In the end, I realized it always was. It was never lost. It was there the whole time waiting for me to reclaim it when I finally stopped ignoring my unconscious relationship with suffering. When I stopped disregarding the damaging patterns that had been woven through my life and instead heeded their lessons, I began the process of untangling from the past.

I am free and alive in the present. I am no longer a seller of secrets but a teller of truth. I stand firmly on solid ground, connected, immersed, and fully here in each moment. I am filled with delight and gratitude. Sometimes, we must allow the heart to break for it to fully open, and when it does, it reveals a bright, shining beacon of light that illuminates the false narrative and prevents our true self from dying.

The Uses of Sorrow

(In my sleep I dreamed this poem)

Someone I loved once gave me
a box full of darkness.
It took me years to understand
that this, too, was a gift.

—Mary Oliver

NOTES

Chapter Two: *False Prophets and Ravening Wolves*

1 Robert Frost, "Nothing Gold Can Stay," in *New Hampshire: A Poem with Notes and Grace Notes* (New York: Henry Holt, 1923), 84.

Chapter Four: *The Primal Scream*

2 Michael Trimble and Dale Hesdorffer, "Music and the Brain: The Neuroscience of Music and Musical Appreciation," *BJPsych International* 14, no. 2 (May 1, 2017): 28–31, https://doi.org/10.1192 /s2056474000001720.

3 Lavinia Rebecchini, "Music, Mental Health, and Immunity," *Brain, Behavior, and Immunity – Health* 18 (October 21, 2018): 100374, https://doi.org/10.1016/j.bbih.2021.100374.

4 William Pole, "The Story of Mozart's Requiem," *The Musical Times and Singing Class Circular* 14, no. 314 (1869): 39–41, https://doi.org /10.2307/3353988.

Chapter Seven: *Into the Thick of Things*

5 Michelle Obama, "Remarks by the First Lady at Hillary for America Campaign Event in Manchester, NH" (Southern New Hampshire University, Manchester, NH, October 13, 2016), https://obamawhite-house.archives.gov/the-press-office/2016/10/13/remarks -first-lady-hillary-america-campaign-event-manchester-nh.

Chapter Eight: *Flipping the Switch*

6 Frank Arjava Petter, *Reiki: The Legacy of Dr. Usui* (Twin Lakes, WI: Lotus, 1998).

7 Einstein to Max Born, March 3, 1947, in *The Born-Einstein Letters: Correspondence between Albert Einstein and Max and Hedwig Born from*

1916 to 1955 with Commentaries by Max Born, trans. Irene Born (New York: Walker, 1971), 157–58.

8   Ben Brubaker, "How Bell's Theorem Proved 'Spooky Action at a Distance' Is Real," *Quanta Magazine*, July 20, 2021, https://www .quantamagazine.org/how-bells-theorem-proved-spooky-action-at-a -distance-is-real-20210720/.

Chapter Ten: *The Arc of the Moral Universe*

9   New York Attorney General's Office, "A. G. Underwood Announces Clergy Abuse Hotline—Part of Investigation into Sexual Abuse of Children Within NY Dioceses of Catholic Church" (press release), September 6, 2018, https://ag.ny.gov/press-release/2018/ag-underwood -announces-clergy-abuse-hotline-part-investigation-sexual-abuse.

10 New York State Senate, Senate Bill S2440, 2019–2020 Legislative Session, https://www.nysenate.gov/legislation/bills/2019/S2440.

Chapter Twelve: *Reclaiming My Power*

11 "Shamanic Healing Services & Resources," The Foundation for Shamanic Studies (website), accessed July 17, 2023, https://shamanism.org/.

Chapter Thirteen: *Quantum Leap*

12 Barbara Ann Brennan, *Hands of Light: A Guide to Healing Through the Human Energy Field* (New York: Bantam Books, 1988).

Chapter Sixteen: *The Devil Is in the Details*

13 Bessel van der Kolk, *The Body Keeps the Score: Brain, Mind, and Body in the Healing of Trauma* (New York: Viking, 2014).

14 *Confirmation Hearing on the Nomination of Hon. Brett M. Kavanaugh to be an Associate Justice of the Supreme Court of the United States*, 115th Cong. (2020) (statement of Christine Blasey Ford, professor of psychology, Palo Alto University, Palo Alto, California, and research psychologist, Stanford University School of Medicine, Stanford, California), https://www.govinfo.gov/content/pkg/CHRG-115shrg 32765/pdf/CHRG-115shrg32765.pdf.

Chapter Seventeen: *Emergence*

15 William Blake, *The Marriage of Heaven and Hell* (1790), https:// blakearchive.org/work/mhh.

ACKNOWLEDGMENTS

To Alex, my life partner, and soul mate, and to my children, you are my greatest gifts in this life, and my love for you is immeasurable. I stand transparent in truth and firmly in resilience and strength and with each of you in the love and deep connection between us, for which I am eternally grateful. Thank you for your unwavering support, hugs, and love ya's.

To my family, I have come to trust in the healing this work has brought, not only for myself but multi-dimensionally throughout our lineage. Clearing these wounds has mended long-standing fractures in the grid that connects us all. Facing the truth and seeking understanding is as difficult as it is incredibly healing, both for oneself and in relationships. Although a difficult journey, wholeness is often the destination. Through this process, I have found it. Please know I hold you all close to my heart.

To my helpers, each one of you seemed to serendipitously arrive at the precise moment I needed you. The support, guidance, and teachings lovingly provided helped to pave the rugged road I traveled to find my true self and will remain in my heart forever. Thank you for being a light in my journey and for decisively standing with me in my darkest moments.

To Rebecca Austill-Clausen, author of *Change Maker, How My Brother's Death Woke Up My Life*, thank you for introducing me to She Writes Press and for your kind words and offers of support.

To Brooke Warner, Lauren Wise, and the women of She Writes Press who create a vital space that empowers, encourages, and supports women's voices and stories, thank you. To the legion of SWP authors who stand with, uplift, and encourage one another: I am thankful to be a part of this amazing community.

To the talented women who provided a master class in writing through their expert advice and direction, Kathleen Furin, book coach, Lorraine Fico-White, copyeditor, and Barrett Briske, proofreader, thank you.

To Tabitha Lahr who designed the perfect cover, thank you.

To Mary Catherine Jones at Voice Over Vermont who constructively and skillfully guided me through the narration of the audiobook, thank you.

I feel incredibly blessed to have the support and encouragement of these amazing women in my life. I am filled with immense gratitude for the invaluable gift of their guidance in bringing this book to life. To friends who kindly read my first drafts and provided insight, support, and encouragement—Lori Lustberg, Jaime Pransky, Danielle Manzello, Aimee Cummo, and Richard Simonds—thank you.

To Michele Gentile, thank you for being an ally in all my endeavors. Your unwavering support has meant the world to me, and I cannot thank you enough for being such a dependable friend through thick and thin.

Thank you to Christine Ambelas, your friendship and consistent support has been invaluable to me, and for that, I am deeply grateful.

To Lynn Massaro, April Owen, Michael Seip, Jeff Sanchez, and families, your kindness has left a lasting impact on my life, and I will always cherish it. Thank you for being there for me.

To Peter Vassil, Louie Gasparro, and the TreeHouse and Sexdigital communities, your support and friendship played a significant role in enabling me to overcome the challenges I faced

ACKNOWLEDGMENTS

and emerge stronger and healthier. Thank you for being an integral part of my healing journey.

To Suzanne Stern: I am much more like a Vermonter, you were right. Thank you for planting the seed.

To friends old and new, each one of you has helped shape my life in unique ways, and I thank you for the love and camaraderie received from the conversations and interactions of friendship that helped me find connection, community, and a sense of belonging.

To friends lost too soon: I'll always remember you.

To the countless musicians, artists, and writers who have influenced me, sparked my curiosity to learn, and brought beauty to my life, thank you.

ABOUT THE AUTHOR

 Kathleen Rose Morgan is a mother, writer, musician, and Reiki Level III practitioner. Originally from Staten Island, New York, she traded ferry boat rides for her kayak when she moved to Vermont where she continues to explore various methods of energy medicine, after-death communication, and the art of healing trauma. Despite enduring adverse childhood experiences that ended her official education prematurely, Kathleen turned to self-education through books, music, mentors, and the cultural offerings of NYC, where she balanced her time between playing guitar and primal screaming and working as a legal administrative assistant. Kathleen's memoir is a testament to the power of confronting a traumatic past with love and understanding and how it can promote personal power, healthy relationships, and community healing for the greater good of the human spirit. For more information, please visit www.kathleenrosemorgan.com.

SELECTED TITLES FROM SHE WRITES PRESS

She Writes Press is an independent publishing company
founded to serve women writers everywhere.
Visit us at www.shewritespress.com.

Indestructible: The Hidden Gifts of Trauma by Krista Nerestant. $16.95, 978-1-63152-799-9. Krista Nerestant endured multiple traumas as a child in the Philippines and a young immigrant in the United States—yet she rose to face every obstacle she encountered with courage and self-love. Along the way, she found success and healing, discovered the hidden gifts of trauma, and eventually became a spiritual medium and inspirational leader in her community.

The Girl in the Red Boots: Making Peace with My Mother by Judith Ruskay Rabinor, PhD. $16.95, 978-1-64742-040-6. After confronting a childhood trauma that had resonated throughout her life, psychologist Dr. Judy Rabinor, an eating disorder expert, converted her pain into a gift and became a wounded healer—a journey that taught her it's never too late to let go of hurts and disappointments and develop compassion for yourself, and even for your mother.

Fortunate Daughter: A Memoir of Reconciliation by Rosie McMahan. $16.95, 978-1-64742-024-6. Intimate, unsentimental, and inspiring, this memoir explores the journey of one woman from abused little girl to healed adult, even as she maintains her relationship with her former abuser.

Baffled by Love: Stories of the Lasting Impact of Childhood Trauma Inflicted by Loved Ones by Laurie Kahn. $16.95, 978-1-63152-226-0. For three decades, Laurie Kahn has treated clients who were abused as children—people who were injured by someone who professed to love them. Here, she shares stories from her own rocky childhood along with those of her clients, weaving a textured tale of the all-too-human search for the "good kind of love."

Being Mean: A Memoir of Sexual Abuse and Survival by Patricia Eagle. $16.95, 978-1-63152-519-3. Patricia is thirteen when her sexual relationship with her father, which began at age four, finally ends. As a young woman she dreams of love but it's not until later in life that she's able to find the strength to see what was before unseeable, rise above her shame and depression, and speak the unspeakable to help herself and others.

Now I Can See the Moon: A Story of a Social Panic, False Memories, and a Life Cut Short by Alice Tallmadge. $16.95, 978-1-63152-330-4. A first-person account from inside the bizarre and life-shattering social panic over child sex abuse that swept through the US in the 1980s—and affected Alice Tallmadge's family in a personal, devastating way.